THE
ULTIMATE FOUNDATION
FOR
REAL LOVE

BY
PETER O. OSAGBODJE

All scripture quotations, unless otherwise indicated, are taken from the *New King James Version of the Bible*. Copyright © 1982 by Thomas Nelson, Inc. Used by permission. All rights reserved.

NASB designated scripture quotations are taken from the *New American Standard Version of the Bible*. Copyright © 1960, 1962, 1963, 1968, 1971, 1972, 1973, 1975, 1977, 1995 by The Lockman Foundation. Used by permission. All rights reserved.

THE ULTIMATE FOUNDATION FOR REAL LOVE
By Peter O. Osagbodje

Copyright © 2007 by Peter Okeremute Osagbodje
ISBN 978-0-9792565-2-3

Published by:
Peter O. Osagbodje
P. O. Box 700971
Tulsa, OK 74170, USA
posagbodje@yahoo.com

Cover design by Melissa Moss, RiverCity Publishing & Digital Printing, Tulsa, OK.

Printed in the United States of America

All rights reserved. No part of this publication may be reproduced or transmitted in any form or by any means for commercial purpose without written permission of the publisher. However, the use of short quotations or occasional page copying for personal or group study is permitted and encouraged. Written permission for any reasonable use of this book will be granted upon request.

Take note that the name satan and other related names are not capitalized, except in the quoted text, because we choose not to acknowledge "it," even to the point of violating grammatical rules.

Table of Contents

Dedication

Acknowledgement

Chapter 1	We All Need Love	7
Chapter 2	What Is Real Love?	12
Chapter 3	Characteristics of Real Love	20
Chapter 4	Real Love Forgives	34
Chapter 5	Value of Real Love	42
Chapter 6	Five Dimensions of Real Love	54
Chapter 7	Learn to Receive the Love of God	55
Chapter 8	Learn to Love God	65
Chapter 9	Learn to Love Yourself	75
Chapter 10	Learn to Love Your Neighbor	88
Chapter 11	Learn to Receive Love From Other People	100
Chapter 12	The Ultimate Solution	106

Appendix 147

Notes 154

DEDICATION

To my wife, Augusta A. Osagbodje, whose consistent love, support, patient, and constructive advice has made the writing of this book possible; and to my children, Gloria and Emmanuel.

ACKNOWLEDGEMENT

It is practically impossible for one individual to produce a product like this. This book has been produced through the combined effort of many people. To all who have contributed to the writing of this book, I say thank you for your help.

I am particularly grateful to my wife and friend forever, Augusta A. Osagbodje, for her encouragement, generosity, patience, and constructive input. Her support made the writing of this book possible. Not only did she support its writing, she also took over some of my responsibilities in the home so that I would have time to write.

To our two children, Gloria and Emmanuel, I say a big thank you for your patience while Daddy was busy writing and reading this book. Your sacrifice is much appreciated. Some of the time I would have spent with you was spent writing this book instead.

I am also grateful to my parents, Mr. and Mrs. Matthew Osagbodje, for giving me a proper education. They had no money, but they did not shy away from borrowing money at an astronomical interest rate to make sure I received the right university education.

I am also grateful to the following people for their assistance in completing this book: Nicki Cooper for proofreading the first draft and the staff of Oral Roberts University word processing department for proofreading the last draft. I am also grateful to all who contributed financially to the publishing of this book.

Last, but certainly not least, I am greatly indebted to God Almighty (Father, Son, and Holy Spirit) whose Holy Spirit inspired me to write this book. His guidance, direction, and still small voice have been very instrumental in the writing of this book. Everything that is of value herein can be attributed to the Holy Spirit.

My Prayer

In the name of Jesus Christ, I pray that all who read this book will be blessed: spirit, soul, body, and financially.

As they read this book, may their lives, especially in the area of their love walk, be changed for the better.

May this book be instrumental in bringing millions of souls into the Kingdom of God. I pray it will help people to restore broken relationships and teach them how to live a life of love.

Amen.

Chapter 1
We All Need Love

No two persons are the same. We are all created differently. Even identical twins are fundamentally different in emotional and spiritual dispositions. We all have different compositions, as well as different desires and aspirations.

However, there is something we all have in common: the desire to love and be loved. It is the most important desire in the heart of a human being. Male or female, old or young, rich or poor, Christian or non-Christian, we all need to love and be loved. It is a normal desire, created in all human beings. We are all created in the image and likeness of God, who is love (Genesis 1:26-27; 1 John 4:8). As a result, we all desire to love and be loved.

This desire originated from the very beginning. Our first ancestor Adam had it, even when he was the only human in existence. It is written, "And the LORD God said, '*It is* not good that man should be alone; I will make him a helper comparable to him'"(Genesis 2:18). We do not know how long Adam was alone before Eve was created. What we do know is that, according to this scripture, even the first created human being had a desire to love and to be loved.

The hunger for love is still very active in us today, and it appears to be growing stronger by the day. We see it, we feel it, and we hear it all around us. It is on the television, on the radio, in newspapers and books, on roadside billboards, and on the Internet. It is in the movies and films we watch, in advertisements, in the news, in secular and even gospel music, and sometimes on the clothes we wear. As far as the world is concerned, no music or film is worth its salt if it does not have a love track or scene in it. Even some Christian movies have subtle love scenes in them. This desire—or should I say cry—for love is everywhere: in the big cities, in the small towns, and in the villages. There is no running away from it.

The tragedy is that this cry for love is not limited to the unmarried or the orphaned. It is coming from virtually every social strata: the married as well as the unmarried, children with parents as well as orphans, the rich as well as the poor, the young as well as the old; all are screaming for love.

There is no doubt that there is a shortage of love in the world today. This should not come as a surprise to us. Jesus said in Matthew 24:12 that in the last days, "And because lawlessness will abound, the love of many will grow cold." That prophecy is prevalent in today's society. The love of many is growing cold by the day. People fall in love one moment, and the next moment it is gone. Love today means one thing to one person and another thing to another person. To some, love is how they feel. For some, love is sex. Some see it as acceptance without corrections, even if they are wrong. A few see it as self-sacrifice. This raises the question of what real love is and how we can experience it.

For several years, I set out to find answers to the above question. I prayerfully and extensively studied the Bible, paying particular attention to scriptures dealing with the subject of love. In the process, I came to the realization that the Bible is not only a book of love (God's love for humankind), but also the unshakable foundation for a true and lasting love (humankind's love for God, as well as our love for each other). I also discovered that to walk in real love, one needs to be totally dependent on the Holy Spirit. As a result, I asked Him to teach me about real love and how to walk in it. The things the Holy Spirit taught me have dramatically changed my own walk of love. There are four things He taught me about love, which I believe are the bedrock to giving and receiving real and lasting love. No matter how spiritual you are, if you lack a good understanding of these things, you will find it very difficult—if not impossible—to come to maturity in your love walk.

1 *Know the value of walking in real love.* In other words, learn to appreciate the benefits of a real love walk. For what you value, you will create time and resources to maintain. The greater value you place on something, the more time and resources you will devote to it.

2 *Know what real love is.* Get to know its nature and characteristics. Until you have that knowledge, you cannot give or receive real love. To actively participate in something, you must know what it is. One of the reasons the love of many is "growing cold" is because people do not have a good understanding of what it means to love someone. We need a good understanding of what real love is in order to walk in it. Otherwise, we will be substituting our own counterfeit understanding of love for the real thing. That is deceptive, and it leads nowhere.

3 *Know the five dimensions of love.* This is the most important key to giving and receiving real love. Love flows in five directions. It is vitally important that you know what is required of you in each of the five directional flows of love. You need to understand the dynamics of each of the five flows and how to react to each of them. Not knowing how to react to the dynamics of each of the five directional flows of love is the cause of most of the disappointment we feel when dealing with people and with ourselves.

4 *Become a person of love instead of trying to walk in love.* In other words, grow up spiritually until walking in love becomes natural to you. While developing your character in this area, work with the Holy Spirit and meditate on the Word until you naturally walk in love no matter the circumstance or situation in which you may find yourself. It is what you become that will eventually determine what you do.

The purpose of this book is to help you grow in love, especially in the four areas listed above. I believe that if you carefully take time to understand the points outlined in this book and diligently apply them, they will change your life forever because they are based purely on the Word of God. When the Word of God is rightly applied, walking in real love is not cumbersome. What we need is to allow the Word to be deeply rooted in us, and we will find it rather easy to experience real love. The answer to walking in real love is in the Word of God, the Bible.

Love is not what you passively learn to do; love is something you actively desire to become. Let me emphasize it once again: It is what you become that will eventually determine what you do. It is what you have on the inside that will eventually rise to the surface. Every tree will bear fruit according to its kind. If you don't like what is coming out of you, change what is inside by changing what you are putting there. If you want to harvest apples, you must plant apple seeds. Don't plant lemon seeds and expect to reap apples.

> "For a good tree does not bear bad fruit, nor does a bad tree bear good fruit. For every tree is known by its own fruit. For *men* do not gather figs from thorns, nor do they gather grapes from a bramble bush. A good man out of the good treasure of his heart brings forth good; and an evil man out of the evil treasure of his heart brings forth evil. For out of the abundance of the heart his mouth speaks." (Luke 6:43-45)

I am confident you can become a person of love if you diligently apply the Word of God to your life. God is not in the business of asking us to do something outside of our human capacity. He has supplied everything we need to accomplish all He requires us to do. His Word and Spirit are the means by which we develop a nature of love.

"Come to Me, all *you* who labor and are heavy laden, and I will give you rest. Take My yoke upon you and learn from Me, for I am gentle and lowly in heart, and you will find rest for your souls. For My yoke *is* easy and My burden is light." (Matthew 11:28-30)

In general, animals instinctively do what is necessary to keep themselves safe and alive.[1] They don't have to strive too hard to do what they were created to do naturally. Fishes don't have to assert too much effort to swim once they have passed the initial stage of learning the technique. They just swim effortlessly because they have the nature of a fish. Birds don't have to assert too much effort to fly once they have passed the initial learning stage; they just fly because they are birds, and they have the nature of birds. The nature of an animal determines what it can do instinctively. As Christians, we must endeavor to put on the nature of God — who is love — so we can walk in love instinctively without too much stress.

Chapter 2

What Is Real Love?

The *Cambridge Advance Learner's Dictionary* defines love as "to have strong feelings of affection for another adult and be romantically and sexually attracted to them, or to feel great affection for a friend or person in your family."[1] In other words, love is feelings for others. This is the world's definition of love. The world has reduced love to feelings. Humanity, in its fallen state, has totally lost touch with what real love is. If you ask ten different people, What is real love?, you may end up with ten different definitions. Even among Christians, there is no clear understanding of what it means. This is why we must turn to the Bible for our definition of real love.

In the Greek language—the language of the New Testament—there are different kinds of love. Unfortunately, in the English version of the Bible, all of these words were translated as love, even though they have slightly (and in some cases significantly) different meanings. Therefore, to understand the Bible's definition of real love, we must be familiar with the different Greek words that were translated as love in the New Testament.

Eros

The Greek word EROS is a term used to describe physical, sexual, or romantic love.[2] It is the root word from which the English words erotic and erotica are derived. It can also be used to describe the kind of infatuations existing among youngsters of opposite sex, which in most cases do not last very long. EROS love does not have to be sinful, as long as it is done within its proper context: marriage.

The word EROS was never used in the New Testament. As far as the Bible is concerned, having sex is not love; it is sexual intercourse—becoming intimate with a person, or knowing that person sexually. It is unfortunate that so many marriages today are built on this kind of love. Such marriages will not last long because they cannot stand the test of time. Youngsters and singles should beware not to mistake this kind of love for real love. Do not get into a marriage relationship on the basis of sexual attraction because sexual attraction will soon fade away. It will not last forever. For most people, sexual attraction usually lasts for only a few sexual encounters; then it fades out almost completely.

This point is very important because many men think that having sex with their wife is what love is about. Many women even encourage their husbands in that thought process by describing sexual intercourse as love. If you describe it as love, your spouse will wrongly think that each time you have sexual intercourse, he or she has fulfilled his or her love obligations. That is not true. One can have sex without love.

STORGE

STORGE is a familial love. This is the kind of protective love that normally exists between parents and their children.[3] This word was never used in the New Testament. However, the related words: PHILOSTORGOS or FILOSTORGOI were translated "kindly affectioned" in Romans 12:10.

PHILARGURIA

The Greek word PHILARGURIA, which appeared about twice in the New Testament, is used to describe the love of money.[4] "For the love [PHILARGURIA] of money is a root of all *kinds of* evil, for which some have strayed from the faith in their greediness, and pierced themselves through with many sorrows" (1 Timothy 6:10). This word can also mean covetousness.

Notice that money itself is not the root of all evil, but the love of it is. Money represents silver, gold, and other material resources; it is a medium of exchange. The Bible teaches that the silver and gold belong to the Lord who created all things (Haggai 2:8). That which was created by God cannot be evil, but the use or exaltation of it can be. It is not the *desire for* money that is evil, but the *love of* it. We all desire money. It is necessary to meet our needs, to do the work of the Kingdom, and to serve the needs of others.

The love of money means to have an insatiable desire for money or to crave it in such a way that it becomes an idol in one's eyes. This happens when one is pursuing money, either instead of or above the things of God. It may also happen when one is willing to do anything—even if one knows it is sin—for the sake of money. When a person puts trust and confidence in money or material possessions instead of in God who is able to provide all things, he or she is in love with money.

Solomon, the king of Israel, started off on a very good note. When God told him to ask for anything, he asked for wisdom instead of wealth. The Bible says that because Solomon asked for wisdom instead of wealth, God not only gave him the wisdom he requested, but also riches and honor (1 Kings 3). Unfortunately, in order to protect his riches, his honor, and his kingdom, he began to marry foreign wives who turned his heart after other gods. The scriptures tell us the sad result: "Solomon did evil in the sight of the Lord, and did not fully follow the Lord, as *did* his father David" (1 Kings 11:6).

The question is, was Solomon's money evil? Definitely not; after all, God gave it to him just as God gave Adam and Eve all that He created. It was Solomon's love for the money and the desire to protect it outside of God's help that led him to evil.

THELO

The Greek word THELO, translated several times in the New Testament as love, means a desire or preference for something. It also means to resolve, to determine, or to take delight or pleasure in something.[5] "Then He said to them in His teaching, 'Beware of the scribes, who desire [THELO] to go around in long robes, *love* [THELO] greetings in the marketplaces, the best seats in the synagogues, and the best places at feasts'" (Mark 12:38-39). In other words, they love their job or office—not because it gives them the opportunity to help develop other people, but because of the accolades and respect that goes with it. This is also the kind of love you may have for a particular kind of sport, clothing, food, or car. There is nothing wrong with this kind of love, but it is not real love. It is rather a liking or preference for something. Don't allow what you like to become bigger and more important than what you truly love.

PHILEO

The Greek word PHILEO and its related forms PHILADELPHIA and PHILADELPHOA describe a relationship between brothers, friends, or to be fond of an individual or an object.[6] It denotes personal attachment, tender affection or kindness towards a person, place, or thing.[6] PHILEO was rarely used in a command for men to love God. It was, however, used as a warning in 1 Corinthians 16:22, "If anyone does not love [PHILEO] the Lord Jesus Christ, let him be accursed. O Lord, come!"

PHILANDROS AND PHILOTEKNOS

PHILANDROS is the kind of affection that a man has for his wife or that a wife has for her husband.[7] "That they admonish the young women to love [PHILANDROS] their husbands, to love [PHILOTEKNOS] their children" (Titus 2:4). Similar to the word PHILANDROS is the word PHILOTEKNOS, meaning to be fond of one's children.[8]

AGAPE

All of the above kinds of love are conditional love. They are not real love because they are natural human love. They exist only in certain conducive environments as determined by the lover. These are all different from and fall short of the real love, which is the God-kind of love. The God-kind of love is AGAPE love. This is love in its purest form. It is an unconditional love.

The word itself is not commonly used in the Greek vocabulary. Rather, the Holy Spirit inspired its usage in the New Testament.[9] This love comes from God. It is the kind of love that is shed abroad in the heart of a believer by the Holy Spirit. It is known only by its action. It is much more than affection and has nothing to do with satisfaction or feelings. It involves a deliberate choice to love irregardless of the person's character, attitudes, or actions. In other words, this kind of love is dependent on the lover's personal resolve, rather than on what the one being loved has done or not done. It does not matter whether you like the person or not, you are to love him or her unconditionally. This is the kind of love that should exist between a man and his wife.

> Husbands, love [AGAPE] your wives, just as Christ also loved [AGAPE] the church and gave Himself for her, So husbands ought to love [AGAPE] their own wives as their own bodies; he who loves [AGAPE] his wife loves [AGAPE] himself. For no one ever hated his own flesh, but nourishes and cherishes it, just as the Lord does the church. *"For this reason a man shall leave his father and mother and be joined to his wife, and the two shall become one flesh."* Nevertheless let each one of you in particular so love [AGAPE] his own wife as himself, and let the wife see that she respects *her* husband.
> (Ephesians 5:25, 28, 29, 31, 33)

> Husbands, love your wives and do not be bitter toward them. (Colossians 3:19)

AGAPE love is much more than *PHILEO* love. The distinction between *AGAPAO* and *PHILEO* can be seen in the following scripture:

> So when they had eaten breakfast, Jesus said to Simon Peter, "Simon, *son* of Jonah, do you love [*AGAPE*] Me more than these?" He said to Him, "Yes, Lord; You know that I love [*PHILEO*] You." He said to him, "Feed My lambs." He said to him again a second time, "Simon, *son* of Jonah, do you love [*AGAPE*] Me?" He said to Him, "Yes, Lord; You know that I love [*PHILEO*] You." He said to him, "Tend My sheep." He said to him the third time, "Simon, *son* of Jonah, do you love [*PHILEO*] Me?" Peter was grieved because He said to him the third time, "Do you love [*PHILEO*] Me?" And he said to Him, "Lord, You know all things; You know that I love [*PHILEO*] You." Jesus said to him, "Feed My sheep."
> (John 21:15-17)

In the first two questions, Jesus used the word *AGAPE*, which from the context of the passage suggests an unselfish love that is willing to sacrifice. However, Peter's answer conveyed a feeling of affection more than the desire to sacrifice. In the third question, Jesus had to come down to Peter's level since it was obvious Peter was yet to fully comprehend the kind of love that God was expecting from him. After Pentecost (Acts 2:1-4) and as Peter's ministry unfolded, he began to understand the kind of love Jesus required from him. We read in Acts 4:18-20, that when Peter and John were arrested by the Jewish establishment and were commanded not to speak or teach in the name of Jesus, they responded, "Whether it is right in the sight of God to listen to you more than to God, you judge. For we cannot but speak the things which we have seen and heard." (Acts 4:19-20).

You see, *AGAPE* love is God-given. It comes from knowing God in a very personal way. You don't have *AGAPE* love by virtue of the fact that all human beings were created by God. Humankind lost the ability to walk in this kind of love when

Adam and Eve fell in the Garden of Eden. This kind of love can only operate in the heart of a believer who has totally surrendered himself or herself to God. In other words, you receive AGAPE love at the New Birth. When you accept Jesus as your personal Lord and Savior, you become a New Creation in Him. The love of God—AGAPE love—is then shed abroad in your heart.

Do not expect this kind of love from an unbeliever. It is unreasonable to expect him or her to love you unselfishly. The Bible says, "We know that we have passed from death to life, because we love the brethren. He who does not love *his* brother abides in death." (1 John 3:14). This scripture tells us that one of the benefits of salvation is the ability to walk in AGAPE love. If we cannot walk in this kind of love, we are still abiding in darkness. It also means that those who are in darkness cannot love the brethren. Unbelievers are still in darkness; they have not yet seen the light. They have not passed from death to life; therefore, they do not have the God-kind of love.

AGAPE love is willing to sacrifice its all for the benefit of someone who least deserves it. This is how God loves us: unselfishly and unconditionally. He sacrificed His very best for us even though we did not deserve it. "For God so loved the world that He gave His only begotten Son, that whoever believes in Him should not perish but have everlasting life" (John 3:16).

This kind of love gives unconditionally. God's love for the world (humanity) is unconditional. He manifested His love for us by sending His Son, Jesus, to die on the cross for our sins, even when we were yet sinners.

> In this the love of God was manifested toward us, that God has sent His only begotten Son into the world, that we might live through Him. In this is love, not that we loved God, but that He loved us and sent His Son *to be* the propitiation for our sins. (1 John 4:9-10)

> But God demonstrates His own love toward us, in that while we were still sinners, Christ died for us. (Romans 5:8)

This is an uncommon love. You cannot find this kind of love in the world; yet, it is the kind of love we all want and need. This is the kind of love we should express toward God; towards our spouse; toward our children; and towards our parents, brothers, sisters, friends, and neighbors—in other words, toward everyone. You can only find this kind of love in God. You get it through an intimate walk with Him because He is love. It is the nature of God, and if you are willing to humble yourself under His mighty hand, it will rub off on you. *AGAPE* love, real love, the God kind of love, is the greatest spiritual force in the world (1 Corinthians 13:13).

Chapter 3

Characteristics of Real Love

Love suffers long *and* is kind; love does not envy; love does not parade itself, is not puffed up; does not behave rudely, does not seek its own, is not provoked, thinks no evil; does not rejoice in iniquity, but rejoices in the truth; bears all things, believes all things, hopes all things, endures all things. Love never fails. But whether *there are* prophecies, they will fail; whether *there are* tongues, they will cease; whether *there is* knowledge, it will vanish away. (1 Corinthians 13:4-8)

What are the characteristics of real love? In other words, how does real love behave? What differentiates it from other kinds of love? Following are some of the characteristics of the God kind of love.

Real Love Suffers Long and Is Kind

Real love suffers long and is kind. The phrase "suffers long" comes from the Greek word MAKROTHUMEO, which means:

> To be of a long spirit; not to lose heart; to persevere patiently and bravely in enduring misfortunes and troubles; to be patient in bearing the offenses and injuries of others; to be mild and slow in avenging; to be longsuffering, slow to anger, slow to punish.[1]

In other words, it is the ability to be patient and to exercise self-restraint in the face of provocation or offense. But it is not enough to suffer long; real love continues to be kind in spite of negative responses from the other person. It means you continue with your usual selfless act or attitude in spite of the other person's continuous attempt to spite you or offend you. You continue to show kindness to the other person, no matter what they do to you. You don't give up. Love never quits. Love perseveres and persists in doing well. Love does not complain or grumble but continues to rejoice and be glad. Love is not easily offended.

The Bible says, "And *whatever* you do in word or deed, *do* all in the name of the Lord Jesus, giving thanks to God the Father through Him" (Colossians 3:17). Love continues in well doing, firmly rooted in the belief that whatever one does, one does it for the Lord. Yes, the benefit goes to the other party (who may or may not appreciate it), but the reward comes from God. He sees your hurt and pains and will reward you in due season. Impatience is not love. Grumbling and complaining are not love. Any unkind attitude toward anyone is not love. Love must be patient and kind. Love does not fight its own battles. Love seeks to overcome evil with good.

No doubt this is a difficult task to do, especially in these days and times when there are plenty of people who thrive on taking advantage of other people. There is so much selfishness, abusiveness, and mean-spiritedness around us. There are many people standing by, watching your every move and response. They are quick to judge you as weak when you begin to demonstrate this kind of love. Society expects you to fight for your rights and to stand up against any oppressive behavior, even if it means fighting dirty. But thank God, we can suffer long and be kind, even in the face of provocation. We can stand for the truth and for what is rightfully ours without fighting dirty or seeking to avenge ourselves. Remember, it's "'Not by might nor by power, but by My Spirit,' says the LORD of hosts" (Zechariah 4:6). Like Paul, you can do all things through

Christ who strengthens you (Philippians 4:13) because He who is in you is greater than he who is in the world (1 John 4:4).

Joseph is an example of how to suffer long. He came to Potiphar's house in Egypt as a slave (Genesis 37; 39). He had every reason to be angry at God, at men, and at himself. However, he did not allow his anger, if any, to get in the way of his blessing. He continued in well doing and continued serving God (Genesis 39). He humbly interpreted people's dreams as the Lord revealed them to him (Genesis 40; 41). The result was that God prospered him, and before long, he became the Prime Minister of Egypt (Genesis 41).

Suffering Long in an Abusive Situation

To suffer long does not mean you put up with an abusive situation. If you find yourself in an abusive relationship, and it is within your power to do something about it, go ahead and do it. However, whatever you do, let it be done in love. What that means is that you don't seek to avenge yourself; rather, you are seeking to set yourself free from that abusive situation. There is a difference between seeking revenge and seeking to set yourself free. The former is vindictiveness and unforgiveness; the latter is self-protection.

How does that work? Whenever you notice that your partner in the relationship (spouse, parents, employers, or even friends) is abusing you; tell him or her, as calmly as you can, that you are not ready to put up with any abusive situation. Then go and report that person to the authorities, your pastor, or someone that has influence over both of you. Let the person know immediately that you are not alone and that you have a bigger family: the Church. Telling the person to stop is not complaining; it is correction. Make sure you follow your pastor's advice or whatever advice you get from someone with better experience than you have. The pastor is there to shepherd you, and he or she will guide you in the right direction.

Real Love Does Not Envy

Real love is not envious or jealous of other people's successes and achievements. Envy is "a feeling of resentment and jealousy toward others because of their possessions or good qualities."[2] It is being resentful because of other people's successes or well-being. It desires to deprive people of what they have. Envy says things like, How come he has such and such? or He shouldn't be driving that car. Jealousy on the other hand, seeks to covet what other people have. It desires to have and keep for itself what the other person has. It says things like, I should be the one having such and such, not him or I should be the one married to such a person, not her.

Envy and jealousy are products of a lack of appreciation for what God has done for you. No matter what your circumstances are, be appreciative of the things God has done for you, and believe God for the things you desire. Appreciate the fact that you are alive, that your name is written in the Lamb's Book of Life, and that God will supply all your needs according to His riches in glory by Christ Jesus.

I recognize that this is not an easy task considering the fact that we live in a fallen world. There is so much unfairness all around us. Many people are getting rich unfairly; hard-working individuals are being laid off with no one to speak for them; consumers are being ripped off daily by greedy merchants. Many are seeing the relationships they have labored for years to build crumble like a deck of cards. All of these have the tendency to breed feelings of personal loss, disappointment, and ill-will towards those we consider unduly favored. However, as Christians, we must not allow disappointments and feelings of personal loss to become envy, jealousy, or hatred.

Envy is not cheap; it is very costly. The price of envy is "rottenness to the bones" (Proverbs 14:30). The Bible warns us that those who practice envy will not inherit the Kingdom of God (Galatians 5:21). We must not be envious of sinners (Proverbs

23:17). If you envy a sinner, you become a sinner. If you envy a righteous person, you are fighting against a child of God. So, no matter who you envy, you have a big problem on your hands. It is much safer to bless them than to envy them. If you find yourself envying someone, learn to pray and bless that person for what he or she has. Then turn around and praise God for what you have and for what He has prepared for you.

Envy can lead to wickedness and even murder. Because of envy, Jesus Christ was delivered up to be killed (Mark 15:10). Joseph's brothers envied him and sold him into slavery (Genesis 37). On several occasions, the Jewish leaders moved against Paul and other Christian leaders out of envy (Acts 13:45). The Bible says that we should love our brothers and not be like Cain, who slew his brother Abel because of envy (1 John 3:11-12).

REAL LOVE DOES NOT PARADE ITSELF

Real love does not brag about itself. It does not boast about what it has accomplished. The Bible says, "Do not boast about tomorrow, for you do not know what a day may bring forth. Let another man praise you, and not your own mouth; a stranger, and not your own lips" (Proverbs 27:1-2). Singing your own praises is not real love because it may cause others to be envious or jealous of you. Learn to handle success with humility. Do not elevate yourself over and above those around you.

This is not to say you should not be ambitious. We were created to be ambitious and to take dominion. You have every God-given right to seek to leave the pack, but try as much as you can not to brag about it because many around you may not have the same drive and enthusiasm as you do.

However, if in the course of your preaching to people and trying to encourage people, the Holy Spirit prompts you to use yourself as an illustration to buttress the truth, then feel free to do so, but don't brag about yourself unnecessarily. If you have to brag, brag about what God has done for you and not what you have achieved.

In the same vein, in an interview or similar circumstance, when you are trying to convince someone you can do the job, you are free to speak boldly of your accomplishments. That is not boasting. In an interview, you have to confidently describe what you have experienced and what you can do, in order to convince the employer you are up to the task.

REAL LOVE IS NOT PUFFED UP

Real love is not arrogant, and it is not inflated with pride. To be puffed up is to have an inflated opinion of one's self-importance. A puffed up individual always thinks he or she is better than others. He or she places a high premium on himself or herself but a very low premium on others. He or she values his or her well-being, family, and properties more than other people's. Puffed up individuals always see themselves at the center of everything. They always think that without them, nothing can be done. That is not true; the truth is that no one is indispensable. Only God, who created and continues to sustain the universe, is indispensable.

Real love requires that you place an equal premium on yourself as well as others. That does not mean you neglect your own needs or the needs of your family. It means you also learn to be concerned about other people's needs as well as your own. We are all equal before God.

REAL LOVE DOES NOT BEHAVE RUDELY

Real love is not rude. In order words, it does not behave improperly, unseemly, unbecomingly, or unmannerly. Real love does not behave indecently towards the person loved. It does not make indecent or inappropriate demands on others. Real love will not put pressure on anyone to do what is contrary to the Word of God. Real love will not entice people to sin or to break the law. For instance, real love will not pressure someone to steal or lie on another's behalf. It will not ask someone to partake in illicit sexual acts. It will not ask someone to willfully disobey God's commandments. Eve did not operate in real love when she offered Adam the fruit of the knowledge of good and evil (Genesis 3:6). Delilah and Jezebel are two examples of people who did not walk in real love (Judges 16; 1 Kings 21).

REAL LOVE DOES NOT SEEK ITS OWN

Real love does not seek its own self-interest at the expense of other people. It is not selfish or self-centered. It is not concerned only about its welfare, but it is also concerned about other people's welfare. Real love sees its existence on earth as an opportunity to make a difference in other people's lives. Real love will always look for opportunities to help others even if it requires some self-sacrifice.

This is the essence of a Christian life: service to the lost. Real love is concerned about how others feel and how they can be helped. Jesus told us that if we wish to follow Him, we must first deny ourselves, and take up our crosses. Only then are we ready to follow Him (Mark 8:34). Real love must deny its own self-interest and put the interest of God and others first. One who is walking in real love must seek:

> The things of God, and what will make most for His honour and glory; and the things of Christ, and what relate to the spread of His Gospel, and the enlargement of His kingdom; and also the things of other men, the temporal and spiritual welfare of the saints: such look not only on their own things, and are concerned for them, but also upon the things of others, which they likewise care for.[3]

The Bible says we should:

> Let nothing be done through selfish ambition or conceit, but in lowliness of mind let each esteem others better than himself. Let each of you look out not only for

his own interests, but also for the interests of others. (Philippians 2:3-4)

Real love requires that we do nothing out of selfish ambition or rivalry. Rather, out of humility and lowliness of mind, we should each value others better than ourselves. We should not only look out for ourselves and those things, which concern us, but we also need to be watchful over the things concerning those around us. We are born to serve God and to serve humanity. Jesus Christ died for all, so that those who live should no longer live for themselves, but for Him who died for them and rose again (2 Corinthians 5:15). Selfishness has no place in the heart of a Christian who is walking in real love.

Real love will not insist on its own rights or its own way. That does not mean you do not recognize your rights, but you do not insist on them. If you get them, fine; if not, give thanks to God and continue in well-doing. Don't allow your rights to become an instrument of offense.

Real Love Is Not Easily Provoked

Real love is not easily aggravated, annoyed, or irritated. It does not get touchy, fretful, or resentful easily. In other words, real love does not flare up at the slightest opportunity. It is not easily provoked or irritated by other people's actions. Real love must have a long fuse. To suffer long means you are not easily provoked.

Love Thinks No Evil and Keeps No Record of Wrong

Real love thinks no evil and keeps no record of wrong or evil done to it. It pays no attention to suffered wrongs. It does not think of or meditate on the evil done to it by another. Real love forgives and forgets. It does not keep a record of past wrongs, neither does it seek revenge for past wrongs.

Those who walk in the God-kind of love will always pray in this manner, "Father, forgive us our trespasses as we forgive those who trespass against us." The Bible says, "For if you forgive men their trespasses, your heavenly Father will also forgive you. But if you do not forgive men their trespasses, neither will your Father forgive your trespasses" (Matthew 6:14-15).

"Love thinks no evil" also means that it is not suspicious of the motives of others. Real love does not impute, reckon, or charge to one's account an evil motive where no evil motive is apparent. On the contrary, real love is quick to give credit and appreciation for good done to it. Good relationships can easily be destroyed where there is suspicion. Relationships must be built on trust in order for them to last long. Where there is lack of trust, there will be lack of love.

Love Does Not Rejoice in Iniquity
It Rejoices in the Truth

Real love does not rejoice in iniquity, corruption, injustice, or unrighteousness. Instead, it rejoices when right and truth prevail. It grieves over its own iniquities, injustice, or unrighteousness. It mourns with sympathetic feelings over the iniquities, injustice, or unrighteousness of other people—even that of an enemy. Love will not rejoice when something bad happens, even to those who have treated it badly.

Jesus said we are to love our enemies, bless those who curse us, and be good to those who hate us. We are to pray for those who spitefully use us and persecute us. Why? Because we are children of God, and God "makes His sun rise on the evil and on the good, and sends rain on the just and on the unjust" (Matthew 5:44-45).

Jesus Christ demonstrated this at the Brook Cedron prior to His arrest and crucifixion. It is written that Judas, having received a band of men and officers from the chief priests and Pharisees, came with lanterns, torches, and weapons to arrest Jesus Christ. Simon Peter, seeing what was happening, drew his sword and smote the high priest's servant, cutting off his right ear. But Jesus rebuked Peter for cutting off the ear of the servant and commanded him to put back his sword (John 18:1-11). In other words, Jesus, instead of rejoicing at what Peter did to one of those who were seeking to take His life, was grieved.

Since love does not rejoice in the iniquities or failures of others, it will not gossip or backbite. Real love will not propagate other people's failures. It does not engage in tongue wagging. This kind of love covers a multitude of sins (1 Peter 4:8). Real love will boldly expose someone else's sins if it is for the good of others but will not expose someone's sin just to cause them embarrassment, shame, or pain.

Real love rejoices in the truth. The word *truth* refers to truth as defined by the Word of God and not by the world. It rejoices when right triumphs over wrong and when good overcomes evil. Real love will be glad to hear the truth, especially the Word of God being preached. It will create opportunity for the truth to reign supreme and will not stand in its way. It will always side with the Word of God, even if it means going against loved ones. Why? Because the Word of God is the truth and it is love.

LOVE BEARS ALL THINGS

Real love bears up under anything. It is not easily frustrated. It withstands disappointment and failures and overcomes circumstances and obstacles to extend hands of fellowship and help, even to those who least deserve it. Real love is like a fireman going into a burning house to rescue the person who deliberately set the fire. This is exactly what Jesus Christ did when He came after us to save us from the consequences of our own sins.

Real love will never stop caring. It will never stop forgiving. It will not hate, despise, or condemn others no matter what is done to it. "For God did not send His Son into the world to condemn the world, but that the world through Him might be saved" (John 3:17). As imitators of God, we too should learn not to condemn but seek to save the lost.

Real love will love its enemies, bless them who curse it, do good to them who hate it, and pray for them who despitefully use and persecute it. However, real love will not allow itself to become an object of abuse. If you are in an abusive situation, seek help.

REAL LOVE BELIEVES ALL THINGS

Real love believes the best of every person; it has faith in people. It believes in people's potential and trusts them to do what God has created them to do. Real love is not gullible, naïve, or blind; it is not suspicious of people's motives. However, real love will always test the spirit and the things people do to make sure they are in agreement with the Word of God. Real love has faith in God and has faith in those whom God has created. It believes all things about the Word of God. It does not doubt the truth of God's Word, even if it cannot understand it. It is grounded on unwavering faith in God and His Word.

Real love will accept and support those whose words and actions agree with the Word but will reject and run away from those whose words and actions are opposed to the Word of God. Someone with real love is:

> Willing to believe all the good things reported of men; he is very credulous of such things, and is unwilling to believe ill reports of persons, or any ill of men; unless it is open and glaring, and is well supported, and there is full evidence of it; he is very incredulous in this respect.[4]

LOVE HOPES ALL THINGS

Real love hopes all things because it believes all things. If you have a strong faith in someone, you will always have strong hope for him or her, and no matter how many times he or she falls, real love will continue to have hope in his or her ability to rise.

When there is no place left for believing good of a person, then love comes in with its hope, where it could not work by its faith; and begins immediately to make allowances and excuses, as far as a good conscience can permit; and farther, anticipates the repentance of the transgressor, and his restoration to the good opinion of society and his place in the Church of God, from which he had fallen.[5]

Real love hopes all things because it believes in God's grace. As Christians, we believe that God can change people and turn their lives around no matter how far they have fallen. In the eyes of God, nobody is lost until they take their last breath. As a result, real love always believes that the worst person in town can change and become the best person. There is an old adage that says, "Man no die, man no rotten." In other words, "A man who is not dead cannot decay." Where there is life, there is hope.

Faith and hope are two of the most important characteristics of love. They are powerful motivational forces. As long as you believe and hope in someone, you will love them and do whatever you can to help them reach their full potential. When these two vital forces are missing, then love becomes dry and dies out naturally. Once faith and hope die, love ceases to exist. This applies to our love for others as well as our love for God.

No wonder 1 Corinthians 13 ends with the following words, "And now abide faith, hope, love, these three; but the greatest of these *is* love" (1 Corinthians 13:13). Faith, hope, and love are connected. They are three of the most important spiritual forces, and they go hand in hand. You need faith to walk in love, you need hope to sustain your faith, faith works by love, and love hopes all things. Therefore, real love is grounded in having the right beliefs (faith) and hope about the people we love.

Love Endures All Things

Real love endures all things without growing cold. This aspect of love refers to perseverance in day-to-day living. Real love does not quit. It does not give up; it perseveres even to the point of death.

Real love will endure discomfort; it will endure afflictions, tribulations, temptations, persecutions, and death itself, especially for the sake of the Gospel. Real love is like a marathon runner who, despite the pain in his body and his desire for fresh air, keeps on running, one step at a time, until he or she crosses the finish line.

Love Never Fails

The last characteristic of real love is that it never fails; it never quits; it never gives up; it never fades out or becomes obsolete; it never comes to an end. In other words, love survives everything. It will survive betrayals, disappointments, failures, and even this heaven and this earth.

> This love never falleth off, because it bears, believes, hopes, and endures all things; and while it does so it cannot fail; it is the means of preserving all other graces; indeed, properly speaking, it includes them all; and all receive their perfection from it. Love to God and man can never be dispensed with. It is essential to social and religious life; without it no communion can be kept up with God; nor can any man have a preparation for eternal glory whose heart and soul are not deeply imbued with it. Without it there never was true religion, nor ever can be; and it not only is necessary through life, but will exist throughout eternity. What were a state of blessedness if it did not comprehend love to God and human spirits in the most exquisite, refined, and perfect degrees?[6]

Faith will change to vision; hope will become enjoyment when we get to Heaven, but love will remain the same. Prophecy, tongues, knowledge, and other spiritual gifts will cease, but love will continue. If anything, it will increase in intensity and become more perfect, but it will remain.

Chapter 4
Real Love Forgives

Forgiveness is a key ingredient in walking in the God-kind of love. It is impossible to walk in love without first learning to forgive and forget. Love and forgiveness go hand-in-hand. The Bible teaches that we should be kind to one another; we should be tenderhearted, forgiving one another as God in Christ forgave us (Ephesians 4:32). The opposite of tenderhearted and forgiving one another is bitterness, wrath, anger, clamor, evil speaking, and malice. All of these are inimical to your spirit and to the Holy Spirit who dwells in you. Unforgiveness will grieve the Holy Spirit by whom you were sealed (Ephesians 4:30). No one wants to grieve the Holy Spirit because to do so will be to your disadvantage.

Ephesians 4:32 says that we are to forgive as God in Christ forgave us. How does God forgive? When God forgives, He also forgets. "I, even I, *am* He who blots out your transgressions for My own sake; and I will not remember your sins" (Isaiah 43:25). Also, 1 John 1:9 says, "If we confess our sins, He is faithful and just to forgive us *our* sins and to cleanse us from all unrighteousness." When God forgives, He remembers it no more. In like manner, we too must learn to forgive and forget and remember it no more. Let the past be the past. Whenever the devil tries to bring back past wrongs or hurts, tell him to get lost. You do not have to pick up the past. Live for the future and not the past.

Jesus said before we ask God for forgiveness, we must first forgive those who trespass against us. If we forgive others their trespasses, God will forgive us our trespasses. If we do not forgive others their trespasses, God will not forgive us our trespasses (Matthew 6:12, 14, 15). In other words, God will forgive us when we wrong Him like we forgive others when they wrong us. This appears to be a very hard saying, but the truth is that those who are called by His name must learn to do as He does.

Beware that you do not have or nurture an unforgiving attitude. Not only can unforgivness ruin your joy, but also your health, faith, and salvation. Absalom, the son of David, king of Israel, is a perfect example of someone who refused to forgive (2 Samuel 13). He refused to forgive his half-brother, Amnon, for forcefully having an affair with his sister, Tamar. As a result, he plotted to kill Amnon and in the process, destroyed the good relationship he had previously had with his father, David. From a human standpoint, Absalom had every right to be offended because Amnon raped his sister. However, God does not operate from a human standpoint; He operates from the spiritual. In the spiritual realm, no matter the level of offense, walking in unforgiveness is never justified. You must understand that you cannot receive God's best if you harbor unforgiveness in your heart.

In Matthew 18:21-35, Jesus gave us a graphic illustration of why it is vitally important that we learn to forgive those who sin against us. It is called the parable of the unforgiving, wicked, or wretched servant. It is a story that started off very good but that ended tragically because of unforgiveness.

The story began with Peter, one of the twelve disciples of Jesus Christ. Peter came to Jesus and said, "Lord, how often shall my brother sin against me, and I forgive him? Up to seven times?" (Matthew 18:21). Peter wanted to know whether it was enough to forgive a brother who continually sinned against him. The reason Peter asked this question was because he realized that offenses will always come. You cannot run away from offenses. As long as you are in this world, offenses will always come. People will offend you, and you will offend them. None of us are perfect yet. Whenever two or more people come together in any kind of relationship, sooner or later they will offend each other. So the question is not whether offenses will come, but rather, how do we deal with them.

Jesus' response to Peter's question was, "I do not say to you, up to seven times, but up to seventy times seven" (Matthew 18:22). The Greek word *HEBDOMEKONTAKIS*, translated *seventy times seven*, actually means "countless times."[1] In other words, we must forgive others as many times as they sinned against us. Jesus then emphasized His point with the illustration found in Matthew 18:23-35. First, He likened the Kingdom of Heaven (the way things are done in Heaven) to a certain king who had many servants. These servants owed him several amounts of money, which he required them to pay. One particular servant owed him ten thousand talents. In today's money, that represents about US$8.4 trillion (Ten thousand talents = 12,000,000 ounces of gold x US$700 per ounce). Since this servant could not pay, the king commanded that he and his family be sold. The servant, moved with fear, fell down before the king and begged for mercy. The king had compassion on him and forgave the entire debt.

Not very long after this, the same servant for whom the king had cancelled the huge debt, saw a fellow servant who owed him a hundred denarii. A denarii was equivalent to a day's minimum wage.[2] If we bring that into the present-day monetary values, a denarii would be worth about US$48 for an eight-hour day. A hundred denarii would therefore be worth about US$4800. The forgiven but ungrateful servant took the other servant by the throat and began to choke him, saying, "Pay me what you owe!" (Matthew 18:28). So the poor fellow servant fell down at his feet and begged him, "Have patience with me, and I will pay you all" (Matthew 18:29). But the first servant refused. He grabbed the poor servant and threw him into prison until he could pay the debt in full.

Unfortunately for the first servant, when his fellow servants saw the way he treated the second servant, they were angry, and they reported him to the king. Then the king called him and said to him, "You wicked servant! I forgave you all that debt because you begged me. Should you not also have had compassion on your fellow servant, just as I had pity on you?"(Matthew 18:32-33). The king was angry, and he commanded that the servant be delivered to the tormentors till he could pay all that was due to him.

Jesus concluded the parable by speaking these words, "So My heavenly Father also will do to you if each of you, from his heart, does not forgive his brother his trespasses" (Matthew 18:35). There can be no better illustration than this. The message is very clear, precise, and directly to the point. Jesus said, in very clear terms, that God will not forgive those who refuse to forgive their fellow brothers or sisters who sinned against them.

Many people find it difficult to believe the spiritual implication of this parable because of the doctrine of justification by grace through faith. It is absolutely true that salvation is by grace through faith in the name of Jesus Christ. That means all who believe that Jesus is the Son of God; that He died on the Cross for our sins and was raised from the dead; and who confess that Jesus is Lord shall be saved. However, salvation itself is not the confession, it is what happens to you on the inside when you genuinely believe and confess that Jesus is Lord. It is not only what you say, but what you become. When you are born again, you are delivered from your old sinful nature. You are then given a new nature, created in Christ Jesus. This new nature is the nature of Christ Himself — the nature of God, who is love. That nature will prompt you to want to do what is right. Your responsibility is to yield to that inner prompting by doing the right thing.

This first servant, in the above parable, either did not take on the nature of the king (the nature of forgiveness) after he was forgiven or he refused to yield to the inner prompting of the new spirit. If you want God to look on you kindly, you must look on others kindly as well. I believe that is fair game. Don't you? Jesus said, "Judge not, and you shall not be judged. Condemn not, and you shall not be condemned. Forgive, and you will be forgiven. Give, and it will be given to you: good measure, pressed down, shaken together, and running over will be put into your bosom. For with the same measure that you use, it will be measured back to you" (Luke 6:37-38). When you refuse to forgive other people their trespasses against you, you are accusing them before God. In the same manner, satan and other bystanders will also accuse you before God.

We all have sinned against God. We all owe Him a debt that requires that we die and go to hell, but God, as an act of love, sent His Son, Jesus Christ, to die on the cross for our sins. In other words, He forgave us our debt. So what right have we to hold someone else's sins against them? The answer is none. We have no right whatsoever to hold their sins against them. If you want God to look upon you kindly, you cannot make people pay for the sins they have committed against you. To insist that payment be made by those who have wronged you grieves the Holy Spirit. It can also cost you your relationship with God.

Release that person right now and let them go. Ask God to heal you of every emotional, psychological, and physical wound that they may have caused you in the past. Pray that God should grant you the grace and strength to forgive them. You can do that right now, and let the healing process begin to take place in you, even as you are reading this book.

How to Deal with Offenses

In Matthew 18:15-17, Jesus gave us a blueprint on how we should deal with those who offend us. Following this blueprint will help to bring physical and spiritual healing both to you and the person who offended you. It is not only the person who is offended that needs healing, the offender needs to repent for their own sake as well. Jesus said, "Woe to the world because of offenses! For offenses must come, but woe to that man by whom the offense comes!" (Matthew 18:7). So when you follow the blueprint below, you are not only doing it for your own sake, but also for the benefit of the offender so that they might have the opportunity to make things right before you and before God.

"Moreover if your brother sins against you, go and tell him his fault between you and him alone. If he hears you, you have gained your brother. But if he will not hear, take with you one or two more, that *'by the mouth of two or three witnesses every word may be established.'* And if he refuses to hear them, tell it to the church. But if he refuses even to hear the church, let him be to you like a heathen and a tax collector." (Matthew 18:15-17)

1 *Tell the person how you feel.* This is very important because more often than not, the offense was not deliberate. Most people who offend you are unaware that they have offended you. If you do not tell them their fault, they will never know to apologize to you. Don't assume that people know the implication of what they say or do to you. It is therefore very important that when you are offended by what someone has said or done, you either go to them in love and let them know how you feel, or you forget it and don't be offended. In other words, if it is too minor to tell them, then forget it and don't consider it an offense. If you learn to apply this principle, it will surprise you how many people will tell you they never intended to offend you in the first place. I have always noticed that more often than not, they will readily apologize and ask for forgiveness. None of us are perfect; we are all striving towards perfection.

2 *If the offender refuses, take one or two people with you and go and see them.* This is usually the case when the offender thinks they are in the right. These are fairly rare cases, but they are generally the worst kind of offense. Some of those who fall into this category will humble themselves and admit their fault when confronted by someone they respect. So make sure that if you have to take someone with you, that he or she has some authority over the offender and is someone the offender will respect. Even better, take someone to whom both of you are somehow accountable.

3 *If offender refuses to hear them, tell it to the church.* This is the case where the person is a Christian like you and you both are submissive to the authority of the church. More often than not, the church knows how to deal with issues of this nature. Not only do they have some expertise in this area, they have the authority of God to mediate between warring brothers and/or sisters.

4 *If the offender refuses even to listen to the church, let him or her be to you as a sinner or tax collector.* These are very extreme cases. I dare say that less than 10% of the offenses you may encounter in your lifetime will fall into this category. However, if you encounter a case like this, Jesus said that you should treat the person as a heathen (sinner or foreigner) or as a tax collector (these are generally despised by the Jews).

The above statement "let him be to you like a heathen and a tax collector" (Matthew 18:17) raises the question of how should Christians treat unrepentant sinners, foreigners, and those ordinarily despised by others. Some Bible scholars have interpreted this statement to mean that we are to excommunicate the offender from the church. I disagree with that interpretation. If we are to excommunicate sinners, foreigners, and those despised in the society because of the nature of their profession, we will end up with empty churches, because even the pastor will be excommunicated. The Christ-like way to treat unrepentant sinners (including those who refuse to apologize for offenses they committed) is to love them, from afar if necessary, and pray for them to come to the knowledge of the truth. However, if they have any leadership responsibility within the church, you may consider releasing them from that responsibility because they are not matured enough to be leaders.

Chapter 5

Value of Real Love

To walk in real love, we must recognize its value. We are rational human beings. We prefer to do what we consider valuable, important, and beneficial. Rational human beings will spend their time doing only those things they appreciate or which they consider valuable; they will rarely spend time on what they consider unimportant or of no value to them. To be rational is part of our human nature; it is very reasonable to spend our limited time and resources on that which is most beneficial to us.

Rational decision making is not only applicable to physical needs or desires; it applies to every aspect of life including religious decisions. For instance, there are many today who have heard the Gospel and have not believed it because they have failed to appreciate the eternal value of salvation. If they would truly understand beyond every reasonable doubt the eternal value of salvation and if they would understand what unbelief will cost them in eternity, they would easily accept Jesus Christ as their Lord and Savior.

The same is true for love. Many do not understand the necessity for love. They have no revelation of how important it is to walk in real love. They have not carried out a cost/benefit analysis of walking in love. As a result, they neither pursue it nor spend time understanding how it should be practiced. Walking in love is very beneficial. Not walking in love is very costly. It could mean the difference between eternity in Heaven and eternity in hell. Following are some of the reasons why we should walk in real love—even if nobody else does.

LOVE IS THE EVIDENCE OF THE NEW BIRTH

One of the evidences of our salvation is the desire in us to walk in real love. The Bible says,

> We know that we have passed from death to life, because we love the brethren. He who does not love his brother abides in death. Whoever hates his brother is a murderer, and you know that no murderer has eternal life abiding in him. (1 John 3:14-15)

Death, in the above scripture, means eternal death. It means living in the kingdom of darkness. It refers to the life of an unbeliever, someone who has not accepted Jesus as Lord. If you are in darkness, you are not born again. On the other hand, life means the New Birth, or salvation. In other words, if you are saved, you will walk in love; so if you are not walking in love, you are not truly saved. Salvation is not only saying, "I am born again." It is not only church attendance or being active in church. All of those are wonderful things to say and do, but true salvation brings about a change on the inside that motivates you to want to walk in love.

I recall an incident that happened to me a few days after I was born again. At the time, I had some on-going problems with a friend. Immediately after I got saved, I knew deep inside that there were several things I had to make right, and I knew one of those things was to reconcile with this friend of mine, even though I felt I was the wounded party. I remember the first Sunday after I answered the altar call in the church. We were preparing to receive communion, when all of a sudden I remembered I had not reconciled with my friend. I was so shaken by the thought of taking communion without reconciling with him that I ran out of the church in fear.

That day, I left him a note asking him to come to my home so we could reconcile our differences. Nobody told me about love; nobody told me I must forgive and forget. I just knew it was wrong for me to continue to bear grudges. It was the Holy Spirit that was working in me. It was my born again spirit; it was my new heart that immediately knew some things had to be put right. That is what happens when you are born again.

If you are born again and you are truly changed on the inside, you will have a strong desire to walk in love. You will not immediately begin to walk in perfect love, but something on the inside of you—the Holy Spirit—will always be prompting you to walk in love. Whether or not you obey the prompting of the Holy Spirit depends on your willingness to obey the things of the Spirit, as well as your understanding of how important it is for you to walk in love.

God is love, and if God dwells inside of you—which is what happens when you are born again—you will desire to walk in love. You may not always walk in love, but that inner desire to do so will always be there. You will love God with all your heart, soul, mind, and strength, and you will love your neighbor as Christ has loved you. When somebody comes to you and says, "How do you know that you are born again?" You can look them straight in the eye and say, "Because I walk in love." The God-kind of love is the evidence that we are truly saved.

If you are saved, you are in the Kingdom of God. In the Kingdom of God, there is no unforgiveness; there is no ill-will towards another person; there is no envy, jealousy, or hatred. There is only love. God has delivered you from the power of darkness and has conveyed you into the Kingdom of His dear Son (Colossians 1:13). As a result, you cannot continue to live as if you are still under the power of darkness. That won't work.

> Therefore, if anyone *is* in Christ, *he is* a new creation; old things have passed away; behold, all things have become new. (2 Corinthians 5:17)

When you got saved, the Spirit of Christ—the Holy Spirit—came into your heart. He brought with Him a new nature, the nature of Christ. One of the characteristics of that new nature is love. That is why the Bible says that the love of God has been poured out in our hearts by the Holy Spirit (Romans 5:5). This love of God that is poured out in our hearts admonishes us to want to do what is right. It admonishes us not to live for ourselves but for Him who died for us (2 Corinthians 5:14-15).

The best and only acceptable way to live for Christ is to obey His commandment. "And this is His commandment: that we should believe on the name of His Son Jesus Christ and love one another, as He gave us commandment" (1 John 3:23). Jesus said, "But why do you call Me 'Lord, Lord,' and not do the things which I say?" (Luke 6:46).

When the Holy Spirit lives in you and is active in you, it is practically impossible to walk around with a clear conscience and continue to have unforgiveness or lack of love in you. When the Spirit of Christ comes into your heart, He will admonish you to forgive. He will admonish you to treat people right. He will admonish you to be kind to people. He will admonish you to walk in love. He will admonish you to do what is right in the sight of God.

For one reason or another, you may not feel like forgiving. You may not feel like treating your neighbor right. You may not feel like showing kindness to other people, but the good news is that love has nothing to do with how you feel. How you feel has nothing to do with love. Love is action; it is how you respond to the prompting of the Holy Spirit that determines love. You may feel like hating someone or retaliating for what they have done to you. That is how you feel; it has nothing to do with love. If someone does something bad to you, you will feel bad, but don't act on your feelings. Do not allow your feelings to control your actions, instead, yield to the prompting of the Holy Spirit and muster all the strength you can to love.

This piece of advice may sound difficult, but the good news is that with God all things are possible. You are not alone in this; the Holy Spirit is with you. "You are of God, little children, and have overcome them, because He who is in you is greater than he who is in the world" (1 John 4:4). The Holy Spirit—the Spirit of Christ—who is in you, is greater than any obstacle, trial, or temptation that may come against you. Always, remember that, like Apostle Paul, you can do all things through Christ who strengthens you (Philippians 4:13).

Love Is a Command

Love is the New Testament commandment. "A new commandment I give to you, that you love one another; as I have loved you, that you also love one another" (John 13:34). This is not a suggestion or an idea; it is a commandment, one that every Christian must obey. No one is excused; everyone must obey it. In the Old Testament, God gave the Israelites a set of laws that they were to follow. In the New Testament, He has given to us one law: the law of love. This one law of love fulfills all the old laws because it encompasses all of them.

If I love my neighbor, I will not commit adultery with his or her spouse. If I love my neighbor, I will not murder him or her. If I love my neighbor, I will not steal his or her property. If I love my neighbor, I will not covet his or her goods. If I love my neighbor, I will not do him or her any harm. As long as I am walking in love towards my neighbor, I will not break any of the commandments (Romans 13:9-10).

This new commandment of love superseded the Old Testament laws because not only did it encompass them, it actually went far beyond them. Comparatively, the new law of love is not equal to the Old Testament laws; it is far greater. All the old laws put together do not equal the law of love. Hebrews 8:7-13 says,

> For if that first covenant had been faultless, then no place would have been sought for a second. Because

finding fault with them, He says: *"Behold, the days are coming, says the* LORD, *when I will make a new covenant with the house of Israel and with the house of Judah — not according to the covenant that I made with their fathers in the day when I took them by the hand to lead them out of the land of Egypt; because they did not continue in My covenant, and I disregarded them, says the* LORD. *For this is the covenant that I will make with the house of Israel after those days, says the* LORD: *I will put My laws in their mind and write them on their hearts; and I will be their God, and they shall be My people. None of them shall teach his neighbor, and none his brother, saying, 'Know the Lord,' for all shall know Me, from the least of them to the greatest of them. For I will be merciful to their unrighteousness, and their sins and their lawless deeds I will remember no more."* In that He says, *"A new covenant,"* He has made the first obsolete. Now what is becoming obsolete and growing old is ready to vanish away. (Hebrews 8:7-13)

This scripture is saying to us that the old covenant, including the old laws, has become obsolete, and that a new and better covenant, including a new and better commandment, has been written in our hearts. Why is the old law obsolete? The old laws are not obsolete in the sense that they have become irrelevant, but rather in the sense that the new commandment encompasses and surpasses them. This new commandment is the commandment of love.

By way of illustration, let us use the seventh old covenant commandment which says, "You shall not commit adultery" (Exodus 20:14). This law is still relevant today as much as it was relevant in the Old Testament. However, in the Old Testament, not only did the law say, you shall not commit adultery, it also permitted the Israelites to stone the guilty man and woman to death.

The man who commits adultery with *another* man's wife, *he* who commits adultery with his neighbor's wife, the adulterer and the adulteress, shall surely be put to death. (Leviticus 20:10)

On the other hand, in the New Testament, the law of love operates differently.

First, the law of love says,

> For the commandments, *"You shall not commit adultery," "You shall not murder," "You shall not steal," "You shall not bear false witness," "You shall not covet,"* and if there is any other commandment, are *all* summed up in this saying, namely, *"You shall love your neighbor as yourself."* Love does no harm to a neighbor; therefore love is the fulfillment of the law. (Romans 13:9-10)

In other words, if you love your neighbor, you will not commit adultery with or against him or her.

Second, the law of love says that if your neighbor commits adultery, you will still extend love, and because of that love, you will not stone him or her to death; instead, you will forgive, just as God has forgiven you.

> Then the scribes and Pharisees brought to Him a woman caught in adultery. And when they had set her in the midst, they said to Him, "Teacher, this woman was caught in adultery, in the very act. Now Moses, in the law, commanded us that such should be stoned. But what do You say?" This they said, testing Him, that they might have *something* of which to accuse Him. But Jesus stooped down and wrote on the ground with *His* finger, as though He did not hear. So when they continued asking Him, He raised Himself up and said to them, "He who is without sin among you, let him throw a stone at her first." And again He stooped down and wrote on the ground. Then those who heard it, being convicted by their conscience, went out one by one, beginning with the oldest even to the last. And Jesus was left alone, and the woman standing in the

midst. When Jesus had raised Himself up and saw no one but the woman, He said to her, "Woman, where are those accusers of yours? Has no one condemned you?" She said, "No one, Lord." And Jesus said to her, "Neither do I condemn you; go and sin no more." (John 8:3-11)

This woman committed adultery, which was punishable by death under the Old Testament law. However, under the New Testament law of love, the people were under divine obligation to forgive her if they wanted to receive forgiveness from the Lord.

"And forgive us our debts, as we forgive our debtors... For if you forgive men their trespasses, your heavenly Father will also forgive you. But if you do not forgive men their trespasses, neither will your Father forgive your trespasses." (Matthew 6:12, 14-15)

LOVE GIVES VALUE TO OUR ACTIONS

The value placed on our works, good deeds, and spiritual manifestations is determined by how much love is behind it. Every act, every deed, and every word must be measured with the barometer of love. If it passes the love test, it will yield spiritual fruit. If it fails to pass the love test, it will be accounted to you as nothing. In other words, without love, what we do or say is vanity upon vanity; a chasing after the wind.

Though I speak with the tongues of men and of angels, but have not love, I have become sounding brass or a clanging cymbal. And though I have *the gift of* prophecy, and understand all mysteries and all knowledge, and though I have all faith, so that I could remove mountains, but have not love, I am nothing. And though I bestow all my goods to feed *the poor*, and though I give my body to be burned, but have not love, it profits me nothing. (1 Corinthians 13:1-3)

If you prophesy or speak in tongues and have no love, you are no more than an empty drum. Empty drums usually make very loud noises. If you have all knowledge, understand all mysteries, and have mountain-moving faith but have no love, you are nothing. If you give away all of your material resources and yourself and have no love, you accomplish nothing. Jesus said,

> "Not everyone who says to Me, 'Lord, Lord,' shall enter the kingdom of heaven, but he who does the will of My Father in heaven. Many will say to Me in that day, 'Lord, Lord, have we not prophesied in Your name, cast out demons in Your name, and done many wonders in Your name?' And then I will declare to them, 'I never knew you; depart from Me, you who practice lawlessness!'" (Matthew 7:21-23)

Faith Works by Love

Love is the catalyst that makes faith work. Without love, faith will not work. Jesus said whatever things we ask for when we pray, we should believe we receive them, and we will have them. However, there is a condition attached to it: walk in love.

> So Jesus answered and said to them, "Have faith in God. For assuredly, I say to you, whoever says to this mountain, 'Be removed and be cast into the sea,' and does not doubt in his heart, but believes that those things he says will be done, he will have whatever he says. Therefore I say to you, whatever things you ask when you pray, believe that you receive *them*, and you will have *them*. And whenever you stand praying, if you have anything against anyone, forgive him, that your Father in heaven may also forgive you your trespasses. But if you do not forgive, neither will your Father in heaven forgive your trespasses."
> (Mark 11:22-26)

The faith that is able to move mountains and receive all that it asks for is the God-kind of faith. It is the faith that is released under the power of the Holy Spirit, and it happens only when we are in right standing with God. We are in right standing with God only when we are obeying His commandment, when we are doing the things that He says.

Scripture teaches that, "*The eyes of the* LORD *are on the righteous, and His ears are open to their prayers; but the face of the* LORD *is against those who do evil*" (1 Peter 3:12). God will answer the prayers of those who are in right standing with Him and will reject the prayers of those who are not. To be in right standing with God, you must learn to walk in love.

LOVE CASTS OUT FEAR

Love casts out fear. When you walk in love, you are in God's perfect will. When you are in God's perfect will you will have nothing to fear. "There is no fear in love; but perfect love casts out fear, because fear involves torment. But he who fears has not been made perfect in love" (1 John 4:18). We have no fear because God abides in us. Greater is He who is in us than he that is in the world. Our future is brighter than our past.

One of my favorite scriptures against fear is Psalm 91.

> He who dwells in the secret place of the Most High shall abide under the shadow of the Almighty. I will say of the LORD, "He is my refuge and my fortress; My God, in Him I will trust." (Psalm 91:1-2)

He who dwells in the secret place of the Most High is one who does the will of God; one who keeps His commandments. God's promise to such a person is this:

> "Because he has set his love upon Me, therefore I will deliver him; I will set him on high, because he has known My name. He shall call upon Me, and I will answer him; I will be with him in trouble; I will deliver him and honor him. With long life I will satisfy him, and show him My salvation." (Psalm 91:14-16)

That should wipe out every form of fear from our lives.

Love Leads to Divine Health

Walking in love leads to good health and not walking in love will adversely affect your health. God said to the Israelites:

> "If you diligently heed the voice of the LORD your God and do what is right in His sight, give ear to His commandments and keep all His statutes, I will put none of the diseases on you which I have brought on the Egyptians. For I *am* the LORD who heals you." (Exodus 15:26)

Since love is the fulfillment of the law, we can rephrase this in terms of the New Testament to mean that if we walk in love, God will not allow any sickness to come upon us. When you walk in love, you are walking in the center of God's will. To be in the center of God's will is to be far removed from a place where satan can touch you. When you are in the center of God's will, you are under His shadow, and as a result, no evil shall befall you and no plague shall come near your dwelling because His angels will encamp around you and your loved ones (Psalm 91:9-11).

> We know that whoever is born of God does not sin; but he who has been born of God keeps himself, and the wicked one does not touch him. (1 John 5:18)

When you set your heart to walk in love, you will not sin, and the wicked one cannot touch you. However, if you do sin, the scripture says, "If we confess our sins, He is faithful and just to forgive us *our* sins, and to cleanse us from all unrighteousness" (1 John 1:9).

Other Benefits

In addition to all the benefits we have addressed so far, there are many others that accrue to us when we love God. God shows mercy unto those who love Him and keep His commandments (Exodus 20:6; Deuteronomy 5:10). He not only shows us special mercy and grace, He also shows mercy and grace to our children and generations after us (Deuteronomy 7:9). If you want God's mercy to be renewed on you and your posterity after you, begin to love God with all your heart, soul, mind, and strength.

God's blessings and promises are for those who love Him (Isaiah 56:6-7; Psalm 145:20; 69:36). Those who love God will receive His blessings and promises on this earth (Mark 10:29-30); and the crown of life and the eternal Kingdom of God in the age to come (James 1:12; 2:5). It is also written that all things work together for good, for those who love God (Romans 8:28-30). As we seek to love God and to please Him, all things will work together for our good. Not only that, but because we love God, He will justify us and glorify us in due season. As we diligently pursue love, we must not forget that scripture teaches us that, *"Eye has not seen, nor ear heard, nor have entered into the heart of man the things which God has prepared for those who love Him"* (1 Corinthians 2:9).

Chapter 6

Five Dimensions of Real Love

There are five dimensions, or what I call directional flows, of real love. These five directional flows of love are: the love of God; love for God; love for self; your love for others; and the love of others for you. In others words, to have a truly satisfying love life, one must learn to receive the love of God, learn to love God, learn to love yourself, learn to love your neighbor, and learn to receive other people's love for you. It is practically impossible to have fulfillment in life if one, some, or all of these five directional flows of love are not operating in your life the way they should.

These dimensions of love are interrelated. Lack of satisfaction with one will have material impact on the others. It is very important to understand these five dimensions of love and the dynamics of how each of them function. Understanding how these different types of love function will help you to know how to cultivate them and how to react to them, especially when any of them become dysfunctional. Sometimes, either through our own choices or through a negative outside influence, some or all of these five directional flows of love can become dysfunctional. The only flow that will never become dysfunctional is the love of God for us. God's love is everlasting. However, our ability to receive that love can easily become dysfunctional. If that is the case, there are things you can do to correct it. The best solution to a defective reception of God's love is to meditate on the Word of God until you become confident in Him. In the next five chapters, I will be discussing each of these five dimensions of love.

Chapter 7

Learn to Receive the Love of God

The first step towards a fulfilled love life is to receive the love of God. This is the foundation for all the other aspects of love. If you have not received the unconditional love of God, you cannot love God, yourself, or your neighbor as much as you should, and you cannot be satisfied with other people's love for you.

The ability to walk in real love comes from accepting God's unconditional love. It is God's grace or enablement that gives us the capacity to love other people unconditionally. It is not by might or by power; it is by the Spirit of the Lord. It is the Holy Spirit who enables us to do the will of God.

A good understanding of the love of God is the key to God's wisdom and grace. Everything that God has done, is doing, or will do on the earth revolves around God's love for humankind. That is the central theme of the Bible: God's love for humankind. Love is the motive for creation. Humankind was created for the heart of God.

We must also understand that the reason for spiritual attacks from the enemy is to get us to think that God does not love us. Whenever you find yourself in a great spiritual battle where the pressure is almost unbearable; where it appears that God is no longer answering your prayers; where it appears that the Word of God is no longer giving you the necessary comfort or direction you need; and where there is repeated adversity and disappointment know that the enemy is trying to get you to deny the love of God.[1] The enemy knows that if he can get you to deny God's love for you, every other thing, including the other areas of love, becomes a problem. If you cannot experience the unconditional love of God, you will find it very difficult to be truly satisfied in life. Your whole life is built on and should revolve around the love of God for you. Only the love of God can truly sustain you in this universe.

How to Know God's Love

The question then is "What exactly is God's love for us?" How do we recognize God's love so that we can receive it without any guilt or shame? Sometimes we debate whether certain things are God's will or not God's will. If we know what the love of God is, we will not debate whether certain things are God's will or not. If it is God's love, it must be God's will. Let's look at some of the ways we know that God loves us.

Creation Motivated by the Love of God

God was motivated to create the world and all that is in the world by His love for humankind. In 1 John 4:8, we see that "God is love." By implication, all of His activities, everything He does including creation, are done because of His love for us. Genesis 1:26-28 says that after God created the heavens, the earth, and all that exists, He said,

> "Let Us make man in Our image, according to Our likeness; let them have dominion over the fish of the sea, over the birds of the air, and over the cattle, over all the earth and over every creeping thing that creeps on the earth." So God created man in His *own* image; in the image of God He created him; male and female He created them. Then God blessed them, and God said to them, "Be fruitful and multiply; fill the earth and sub-

due it; have dominion over the fish of the sea, over the birds of the air, and over every living thing that moves on the earth." (Genesis 1:26-28)

It is written that, "But whoever has this world's goods, and sees his brother in need, and shuts up his heart from him, how does the love of God abide in him?" (1 John 3:17). This scripture applies to God as much as it applies to us. God cannot love us and at the same time shut up His heart from our needs. One way we know that He truly loves us is because He supplies our needs according to His riches in glory by Christ Jesus (Philippians 4:19). Love is all about giving. Love's desire is always to give the very best to the one being loved. When you love someone, you want to give him or her what you know he or she needs; what is good for him or her.

Not only did God give us all He created, He also created us in His own image and likeness. We are the only creature that was created as such. We are very special to God, and I believe God looks upon us as an extension of Himself. When something is special, you do whatever it takes to protect and guide it. We are special to God. That explains why He moved heaven and earth to bring us salvation. The significance of this is that you should see yourself as a special being created in the image and likeness of God the Father, and because you are special to Him, He is always there for you. His love for you is unquenchable. No one in his or her right senses hates his or her flesh. How much more God? You are of God's image and likeness, and His love for you is everlasting.

"Can a woman forget her nursing child, and not have compassion on the son of her womb? Surely they may forget, yet I will not forget you. See, I have inscribed you on the palms of My hands; your walls are continually before Me."
(Isaiah 49:15-16)

When I consider Your heavens, the work of Your fingers, the moon and the stars, which You have ordained, what is man that You are mindful of him, and the son of man that You visit him? For You have made him a little lower than the angels, and You have crowned him with glory and honor. You have made him to have dominion over the works of Your hands; You have put all things under his feet. (Psalm 8:3-6)

God will not forget you because you are engraved in the palms of His hands, and you are always in His sight. His eyes are always upon you; they will never be withdrawn from you. God thinks about us everyday. We are His most valuable possession. Without us, all that He created would be meaningless. The land, the sea, the sky, the sun, the moon, the animals, the plants, and all other creatures have meaning only because they were created for humankind to enjoy.

The next time you look at yourself in the mirror, I challenge you to look beyond your flesh, and try to look at your spirit. Your spirit is the real you that was created in the image and likeness of God. It is the real you that was born again the moment you accepted Jesus Christ as your personal Lord and Savior. That is what God is after. It is the part of God that became you and was lost because of sin then was brought back to life when you received Christ into your heart.

This knowledge should inspire you to step out in faith and become the best that God wants you to be in life. Go out and take dominion over the fish of the sea, the birds of the air, the cattle of the field, the creeping things, and all that is on the earth. Be confident; you have God on your side. He is for you one hundred percent. Remember, if you succeed in the good things, God succeeds. If you excel, God excels. Do whatever you are called to do heartily as unto the Lord.

Aim for the top because you can be all that God wants you to be in Jesus name. Say no to depression, inferiority, weepiness, and self-pity. Instead, get down on your knees and ask God to show you how to overcome through Christ Jesus. God wants you to prosper in all that you do. His utmost desire is that you prosper and be in health, even as your soul prospers

(3 John 2). God does not want you to be poor; He wants you to be rich. God does not want you to be sick; He wants you to be in divine health. God wants you and your loved ones to have all that you need to live a joyful, happy, and fulfilled life. I pray, in the mighty name of Jesus Christ, that the Lord will visit you as you are reading this book, and that His love for you will be made real in your heart, and that His blessings will become evident in your life forever.

SALVATION: A DEMONSTRATION OF GOD'S LOVE

The second way God has manifested His love toward us is through the death of His Son, Jesus Christ.

> But God demonstrates His own love toward us, in that while we were still sinners, Christ died for us. (Romans 5:8)

God's love for us is salvation. He demonstrated His love for us by sacrificing His only begotten Son for the sin of world. It is the love of God for you, for me, and for all of humanity that compelled Him to sacrifice His only begotten Son, Jesus Christ, on the cross of Calvary. Jesus died to pay the full price for our sins. He took your place as a sinner so that you may become the righteousness of God in Christ Jesus.

That is real love. He did not send His Son into the world because we loved Him or because we deserved it. He did it all because of His great love for us (1 John 4:9-10). God's love for you has nothing to do with your goodness or lack thereof. It does not matter who you are or what you may have done or will do; God loves you and will continue to love you. His love is universal; it is available to all who will receive it.

> "For God so loved the world that He gave His only begotten Son, that whoever believes in Him should not perish but have everlasting life. For God did not send His Son into the world to condemn the world, but that the world through Him might be saved." (John 3:16-17)

God is not sitting in Heaven, judging and condemning sinners, and looking for people to throw into hell. Instead, God is actively seeking the lost and looking to deliver those who will call upon His name. It is written, "For the eyes of the LORD run to and fro throughout the whole earth, to show Himself strong on behalf of *those* whose heart is loyal to Him" (2 Chronicles 16:9).

Therefore, whenever you sin against God, do not run away from Him; run to Him. The Bible says, "If we confess our sins, He is faithful and just to forgive us *our* sins and to cleanse us from all unrighteousness" (1 John 1:9). God is a merciful God, and He is "not willing that any should perish but that all should come to repentance" (2 Peter 3:9).

GOD IS LONGSUFFERING, MERCIFUL, AND COMPASSIONATE

But You, O Lord, *are* a God full of compassion, and gracious, longsuffering and abundant in mercy and truth. (Psalm 86:15)

If You, LORD, should mark iniquities, O Lord, who could stand? But there is forgiveness with You, that You may be feared. (Psalm 130:3-4)

"But if a wicked man turns from all his sins which he has committed, keeps all My statutes, and does what is lawful and right, he shall surely live; he shall not die. None of the transgressions which he has committed shall be remembered against him; because of the righteousness which he has done, he shall live. Do I have any pleasure at all that the wicked should die?" says the Lord GOD, "and not that he should turn from his ways and live?" (Ezekiel 18:21-23)

God's love is demonstrated in His patience, mercy, and compassion. God is gracious, longsuffering, and abounds in mercy. He is slow to anger and to mete out judgment. If God were to deal with us on the basis of what we have done or not done, no one would be able to stand before Him. If He were to judge us on the basis of our iniquities, we would all be found guilty, "for all have sinned and fall short of the glory of God" (Romans 3:23).

When Adam and Eve sinned against God in the Garden of Eden, they ran and hid themselves among the trees. Nevertheless, God, in His love, came looking for them and gave them clothes to wear and even preserved their lives for over 900 years. It was God's longsuffering, mercy, and compassion that made Him to persevere for the next four thousand years as He unfolded His plan of salvation for the redemption of sinful humankind. In spite of the countless number of times that humankind ignorantly tried to frustrate God's attempts to redeem us, God persevered. He never gave up; He kept on coming after us. That is longsuffering, mercy, and compassion. It is all because God's love for us is everlasting.

Time to Recognize the Love of God

Like the psalmist in Psalm 103, it is time for us to recognize the fact that God is the one who heals our diseases and redeems our lives from destruction. He crowns us with loving kindness and tender mercies. He satisfies our mouth with good things so that our youth is renewed like the eagle's. He executes righteousness and justice for the oppressed. He is merciful and gracious, slow to anger, and abounding in mercy towards us. He does not strive with us nor is He angry with us forever. He has not dealt with us according to our sins nor punished us according to our iniquities. Instead, He has shown us mercy over and over again.

So the question is not whether God loves you. The question is do you recognize that He loves you and are you willing to receive God's love? Better still, do you understand the depth of His love towards you? This is the most important key to walking in real love. The degree to which you understand, appreciate, and receive the love of God for you will determine the degree to which you can love and be loved by others. In most

62 | The Ultimate Foundation for Real Love

cases, if someone's love life is distorted, it is because he or she has yet to accept the true love of God.

To walk in real love, you must first recognize the love of God for you. It is the foundation for all other love, the rock on which other love stands. Until you have a full and complete dosage of this love, you will never be fulfilled in life, and you can never have true love for others or receive other people's love. You cannot walk in real love until you are fully secured in the fact that God truly loves and cares for you.

Before proceeding any further, let me ask you this question. Have you accepted Jesus Christ as your Lord and Savior? Do you have a personal relationship with God? If not, this is a perfect opportunity to do so right now. What you have to do is believe that Jesus is the Son of God, that He died for your sins, and that He rose again from the dead. Repent of your sins, and ask Him to forgive you. Then ask Jesus to come into your heart, and confess that Jesus is your Lord and Savior.

> But what does it say? *"The word is near you, even in your mouth and in your heart"* (that is, the word of faith which we preach): that if you confess with your mouth the Lord Jesus and believe in your heart that God has raised Him from the dead, you will be saved. For with the heart one believes to righteousness, and with the mouth confession is made unto salvation. For the Scripture says, *"Whoever believes on Him will not be put to shame."* For there is no distinction between Jew and Greek, for the same Lord over all is rich to all who call upon Him. For *"whoever calls upon the name of the LORD shall be saved."* (Romans 10:8-13)

Please pray this prayer of salvation right now, and your life will never be the same again; it will change for the better.

Prayer of Salvation

"Dear God, I recognize that I have sinned against You and against other people. Please forgive my sins. I repent of them. I believe in my

heart that Jesus Christ was crucified for my sins. I believe in my heart that You raised Him from the dead. I confess with my mouth that Jesus is Lord. He is my Lord and my Savior. Jesus, You are my Lord and my Savior.

"Come into my heart Lord Jesus. Fill me with Your Holy Spirit. Create in me a clean heart and a renewed and steadfast spirit. Cast me not away from Your presence. Restore unto me the Joy of Your salvation. And help me to love You with all of my heart, with all of my soul, with all of my mind, and with all of my strength in Jesus' Name I pray.

"Thank You, Father God, I believe that from now on I am a new creature. I am created in Christ Jesus for good works. From now on, God, You are my Father, and I will live for You all the days of my life. In Jesus' Name, Amen."

If you prayed the above prayer, you are born again. From now on, diligently seek the Lord and learn to receive His love for you. You are now the righteousness of God in Christ Jesus. That means your old sinful nature and your past sins have been purged, and you have been given a new nature, a new spirit—a spirit that is alive to God.

> Therefore, if anyone *is* in Christ, *he is* a new creation; old things have passed away; behold, all things have become new. Now all things *are* of God, who has reconciled us to Himself through Jesus Christ, and has given us the ministry of reconciliation, that is, that God was in Christ reconciling the world to Himself, not imputing their trespasses to them, and has committed to us the word of reconciliation. Now then, we are ambassadors for Christ, as though God were pleading through us: we implore you on Christ's behalf, be reconciled to God. For He made Him who knew no sin to be sin for us, that we might become the righteousness of God in Him. (2 Corinthians 5:17-21)

If you are not presently attending church, go and find one where you feel welcome. Tell the pastor or one of his associates that you have recently accepted Jesus as your Lord. They will guide you appropriately. Also, please feel free to write us a letter or send us an email, and we will send some materials that will help you in your Christian walk. Our address is located on the copyright page of this book.

In chapter twelve of this book, I have compiled some scriptures that will better help you to understand, recognize, and receive the love God has for you. Meditate on these scriptures on a regular basis until they are deeply rooted in your heart. They will not only renew your mind, but they will also build within you a natural consciousness of the fact that God loves you, even if nobody else does.

Chapter 8

Learn to Love God

The second dimension to a fulfilled love life is to learn to love God. Just as God loves us, it is a must that we love Him if we are to have a truly fulfilled life. There is no fulfillment where there is no love for God. The greatest commandment is to love God with all of your heart, all of your soul, all of your mind, and all of your strength. There is no greater love than this.

Then one of the scribes came, and having heard them reasoning together, perceiving that He had answered them well, asked Him, "Which is the first commandment of all?" Jesus answered him, "The first of all the commandments is: *'Hear, O Israel, the LORD our God, the LORD is one. And you shall love the LORD your God with all your heart, with all your soul, with all your mind, and with all your strength.'* This is the first commandment. And the second, like *it, is* this: *'You shall love your neighbor as yourself.'* There is no other commandment greater than these.' So the scribe said to Him, "Well said, Teacher. You have spoken the truth, for there is one God, and there is no other but He. And to love Him with all the heart, with all the understanding, with all the soul, and with all the strength, and to love one's neighbor as oneself, is more than all the whole burnt offerings and sacrifices.' So when Jesus saw that he answered wisely, He said to him, "You are not far from the kingdom of God." (Mark 12:28-34)

How do you love God with all your heart, with all your soul, with all your mind, and with all your strength?

How to Love God with All Your Heart

Know God as Father

To love God with all of your heart means first and foremost, you must know God as your Father. To know God as your Father is to be spiritually alive to God and to accept Him as your heavenly Father. God is a God of the living not of the dead. To be spiritually alive to God is to have a personal relationship with Him. In other words, it means that you must be born again. If you are not born again, you cannot love God with all of your heart.

To be born again is to allow the Holy Spirit to come into your heart and bring it alive to God. It means to be born of the Spirit or to be born of God. It is something that happens spiritually when you invite Jesus Christ to come into your heart. The Holy Spirit, who is also called the Spirit of Christ, creates in you a new spirit, and you become a new creation, created in Christ Jesus (2 Corinthians 5:17; Ephesians 2:10). To be *born again*, to be *born of the Spirit*, and to be *born of God* all mean the same thing: you are now a child of God.

> For as many as are led by the Spirit of God, these are sons of God. For you did not receive the spirit of bondage again to fear, but you received the Spirit of adoption by whom we cry out, "Abba, Father." The Spirit Himself bears witness with our spirit that we are children of God, and if children, then heirs—heirs of God and joint heirs with Christ. (Romans 8:14-17)

But when the fullness of the time had come, God sent forth His Son, born of a woman, born under the law, to redeem those who were under the law, that we might receive the adoption as sons. And because you are sons, God has sent forth the Spirit of His Son into your hearts, crying out, "Abba, Father" Therefore you are no longer a slave but a son, and if a son, then an heir of God through Christ. (Galatians 4:4-7)

As a child of God, you have access to His presence at any time, and you can worship Him in spirit and in truth (John 4:23). There is no more fear and no more hindrance between you and God. His Spirit now lives in you permanently.

Make God Your First Priority

To love God with all your heart is to put God and His Word first place in your daily life. If we say we love God with all our heart, then God must be first and foremost in our daily activities. You consult Him first before you make any key decisions in life. Your decisions must be based on the Word of God; they must agree with the Word. There should be no idols or other gods in your life. The desire to please God must be the chief determinant of what you do. He has all of your heart, and anything you do should be because your heart tells you it is in accordance with God's will for you.

It also means you love nothing else in comparison to God, and you love other things or persons only in reference to the love you have for God. In other words, you love God above any other thing, and you love other things only because it is a demonstration of your love for God, or because it helps you to love God. For instance, I love my neighbor because God asks me to do so, and because it is actually a demonstration of my love for God. I love my job because it helps me to demonstrate my love to God and to those I love. I love going to baseball games because it relaxes my body, which is the temple of God.

What that means is that if there is a conflict between my love for God and my love for other people or things, my love for God must prevail because my love for other people or things is a demonstration of my love for God. In other words, to love other people or things is a means by which I demonstrate my love for God, which is the ultimate end. As a result, it will be wrong for me to allow the means (love for other people or things) to become more important than the end (love for God). If the end (love for God) requires that I give up the means (love for other things) I must be quick to do so.

Worship God

To love God with all your heart is to worship Him. If you love God with all your heart, you will seek to worship Him wholeheartedly and regularly. Worship should be both personal and corporate. It is good to find a regular time to worship God; both in your own private setting and with your family. Also, on a regular basis, go to church and other Christian meetings to worship the Lord with your brothers and sisters in Christ.

What is worship? The word *worship* in both the Old Testament Hebrew and the New Testament Greek means to bow down in reverence and adoration before the object of worship. Therefore, to worship God is to bow down in reverence and adoration before Him. The heart, the soul, the pride, and the five physical senses (the flesh) must prostrate in reverence, in adoration, and in total submission to the God who created the whole universe and in whom we live and breathe.

Worship is much more than singing hymns or praise songs to God. Some properly composed hymns or praise songs, if sung intelligently and reverentially, will lead to worship or may be used to express heartfelt worship. Nevertheless, true worship extends far beyond just singing. True worship is a submissive response to God in reverence, adoration, prayer, praise, and offering. This heartfelt submission must be demonstrated in an outward physical expression such as bowing, kneeling, or lifting up of hands.

The Bible has plenty examples of what it means to worship God. Whenever Moses came into the presence of God, he always bowed his head towards the ground to worship the God of all creation. The same is true for the kings and people of Israel. They always bowed down to worship God. In Heaven, the angels, the elders, and the four living creatures are continuously prostrated before the throne of God in worship. When we get to Heaven, we will also have to prostrate before God to worship Him; so we might as well start now.

So Moses made haste and bowed his head toward the earth, and worshiped. (Exodus 34:8.)

When all the children of Israel saw how the fire came down, and the glory of the LORD on the temple, they bowed their faces to the ground on the pavement, and worshiped and praised the LORD, saying: "For *He* is good, for His mercy *endures* forever." (2 Chronicles 7:3)

And when they had finished offering, the king and all who were present with him bowed and worshiped. Moreover King Hezekiah and the leaders commanded the Levites to sing praise to the LORD with the words of David and of Asaph the seer. So they sang praises with gladness, and they bowed their heads and worshiped. (2 Chronicles 29:29-30)

All the angels stood around the throne and the elders and the four living creatures, and fell on their faces before the throne and worshiped God, saying: "Amen! Blessing and glory and wisdom, Thanksgiving and honor and power and might, Be to our God forever and ever. Amen." (Revelation 7:11-12)

How to Love God with All Your Soul

Be passionate about God

To love God with all of your soul means your whole being should be passionate only about God, His Word, and all that He stands for. The emphasis here is not only on *soul*; it is also on *all*. By implication you cannot share your passion with any thing apart from God. He is thrilled when people are passionate about Him. The Bible says, "Delight yourself also in the LORD, and He shall give you the desires of your heart" (Psalm 37:4). Being passionate about God means you do only those things He desires for you to do.

For example, you are free to go to a baseball game, to go on vacation, to take your family out for dinner, or to take a trip out of town to just go and relax. But you must recognize that all of these are secondary to your love for God. You must see them as part of what God desires for you. He wants you to take time off work to relax. He requires that you take very good care of your family and your body. As you do these things, however, you must be careful not to allow them to become your god.

Be willing to sacrifice comfort

To love God with all your soul also means one is ready to give up life, give up comfort, and suffer persecution, pain, and torment rather than dishonor God. There is nothing wrong with being comfortable. As a matter of fact, God's ultimate will for us as His children is that we live in comfort. However, we must use life's comfort and other conveniences to serve, honor, and glorify God. And if it becomes necessary to give up those comforts and conveniences, we must be willing to do so.

Daniel and the three Hebrew boys are good examples. They were ready to give up comfort to face death rather than dishonor God. Paul and several of the Apostles also demonstrated this kind of love when they left the comfort of their homes and country to carry the Gospel to other nations. This kind of love will make you endure hardship for the sake of the Gospel.

SURRENDER YOUR EMOTIONS TO GOD

To love God with all of your soul also means that you surrender your emotions to God. Don't be controlled by your feelings and emotions. Instead, let the Word of God control you. Even if you are single and alone, don't get caught up in the pity me party. Instead, use your God-given love to show love to those He may bring across your path. As you step out to love, I believe you will not remain single long because you will reap what you sow. As you sow love, you will reap love.

HOW TO LOVE GOD WITH ALL YOUR MIND

LEARN ABOUT GOD

To love God is to seek to know more about Him. When we love a person, we want to know everything possible about him or her. The same is true of our love for God. If we love Him, we will have a deep desire to know as much about Him as we can. My heart's desire is to know everything that is humanly possible about my God.

To learn more about a person, you need to spend time with him or her, getting to know his or her dreams, goals, aspirations, as well as the more superficial things. It is the same with God. To learn about God, you need to spend quality time with Him in prayer, fellowship, worship, and in reading about Him.

There are several resources available to us today that can help us know more about God: the Bible, commentaries, books, tapes, CDs, DVD's, and several others. The most valuable of all of these resources is the Bible. As a matter of fact, there is no substitute or alternative source to the Bible from which we can learn about God. All other sources are designed to help us better understand the Bible and not to replace it. The Bible is

God's revelation of Himself. In it we read about God's dealings with humankind; human nature and failures; and God's direction and guidelines for living. In the Bible, we also learn of God, about His nature, His love, His Son, and His plans for us.

Since the time when the first five books of the Bible were written, the scripture has always been the most valuable source for learning about God. The Lord told Joshua not to allow the Book of the Law to depart from his mouth but that he should meditate on it day and night (Joshua 1:8). On several occasions, when the Jews confronted Jesus about His identity, He referred them back to the scripture (John 5:39). Paul and the other Apostles used the scripture (the Old Testament) to preach about God and about Jesus Christ.

Therefore, to learn about God, you must spend quality time in studying the Bible. To you, learning about God should be an act of worship. Marvin R. Wilson, in his book *Our Father Abraham: Jewish Roots of the Christian Faith*, wrote, "The Bible, however, teaches that study ought to be above everything else, an act of worship, one of the highest ways by which a person can glorify God."[1]

RENEW THE MIND

To love God with all our mind is to make a conscious effort to renew it. To *renew the mind* means to replace old sinful, worldly, and vain thoughts with God's truth by reading, hearing, and meditating on the Word of God. It means learning how to think good and pure thoughts. Loving God with our mind means we will meditate on His Word day and night. We have no business using our mind to meditate on evil and wicked thoughts. We must put our mind to work for God and not for the devil. Our reasoning should line up with the Word of God. We cannot say we love God with all our mind if we persist in having a worldview that is contrary to His Word.

God's ways are not our ways, and God's thoughts are not our thoughts. Until our ways and thoughts are in line with His

Word, we cannot say we truly love Him with our entire mind. We must get our thinking strengthened by the Word of God if we truly want to love Him with all our mind. There is a very good book on the subject of renewing the mind, which I believe will be a tremendous help to you. It helped me a lot, and it is helping me still. The title of the book is *What's On Your Mind?* It was written and published by Merlin Carothers, and at the time of this writing, it has sold over 13,000,000 copies.

How to Love God with All Your Strength

Active Involvement in the Work of the Kingdom

To love God with all your strength means to live for Him. This means one of two things. It may mean you become a full-time minister of the Gospel, or it may mean you actively support the work of God's ministry. For some people, it may mean both. The Bible says,

> And He died for all, that those who live should live no longer for themselves, but for Him who died for them and rose again. Now all things *are* of God, who has reconciled us to Himself through Jesus Christ, and has given us the ministry of reconciliation, that is, that God was in Christ reconciling the world to Himself, not imputing their trespasses to them, and has committed to us the word of reconciliation. Now then, we are ambassadors for Christ, as though God were pleading through us: we implore *you* on Christ's behalf, be reconciled to God. (2 Corinthians 5:15, 18-20).

As Christians, we are not of this world. We are citizens of heaven. However, we are left here on earth to continue the ministry of our Lord and Savior, Jesus Christ. His ministry is to seek and save the lost. We are His ambassadors, and our responsibility is to preach, teach, and heal the sick. God's heart's desire is that no one should perish but that all should come to repentance, and that requires the word of salvation to be preached to all. Every Christian has a responsibility — a role to play in getting the Gospel out to unbelievers. Your role depends on what God has called you to do.

Maybe He has called and empowered you to be an accountant, lawyer, doctor, banker, teacher, policeman, or businessman. You should see your career as your calling and do it heartily as unto the Lord. Not only that you may please your boss but that you may please God. First, let your place of work become a mission field for you. Second, from that calling (job or career), God expects you to pay your bills and feed your family. He also expects you to support the work of His Kingdom by giving tithes, offerings, and sowing seeds into Christian churches and ministries that are committed to winning souls and equipping saints for the work of the Kingdom.

Without the support of people like us, the Gospel cannot be preached. God is depending on Christians—you and I—to preach the Gospel. If we don't do it, it will not be done. So to love God with all your strength, you must be actively involved in the work of the Kingdom. Be actively involved in getting the good news of salvation out to the uttermost parts of the earth.

> Having then gifts differing according to the grace that is given to us, *let us use them:* if prophecy, *let us prophesy* in proportion to our faith; or ministry, *let us use it* in *our* ministering; he who teaches, in teaching; he who exhorts, in exhortation; he who gives, with liberality; he who leads, with diligence; he who shows mercy, with cheerfulness. (Romans 12:6-8)

If you are not in full-time ministry, consider yourself as being in the GIVING ministry. Seek to give actively and generously into the work of the Gospel. As you give, God will begin to enlarge your territory and your finances because He knows for what purpose you are seeking to prosper. Let giving be to you what preaching and teaching are to a pastor.

Chapter 9

Learn to Love Yourself

The third dimension to walking in real love is to learn to love yourself. Having the right thoughts and appreciation about who you are is vital to your well-being, especially as it relates to loving and being loved. If you love yourself, you will find it very easy to walk in the other four areas of love. If you love yourself, you will find it easier to love God and to love other people. You will also find it easier to appreciate the things that have been done for you.

Have the Right Self-Image

Are you happy with yourself, or do you despise something about how you look? There is no reason in this world why you should despise yourself because as long as you are alive, God can change your circumstance and situation for the better. You may be thinking that you do not amount to much, but in the eyes of God, you are very valuable. If you are having difficulty loving yourself, turn your eyes from your problems and begin to look to the Word of God for His solutions. The story of the woman who had the flow of blood in Mark 5:25-34 is a good example of how God can suddenly change circumstances for the better.

> Now a certain woman had a flow of blood for twelve years, and had suffered many things from many physicians. She had spent all that she had and was no

better, but rather grew worse. When she heard about Jesus, she came behind *Him* in the crowd and touched His garment; for she said, "If only I may touch His clothes, I shall be made well." Immediately the fountain of her blood was dried up, and she felt in *her* body that she was healed of the affliction. And Jesus, immediately knowing in Himself that power had gone out of Him, turned around in the crowd and said, "Who touched My clothes?" But His disciples said to Him, "You see the multitude thronging You, and You say, "Who touched Me?" And He looked around to see her who had done this thing. But the woman, fearing and trembling, knowing what had happened to her, came and fell down before Him and told Him the whole truth. And He said to her, "Daughter, your faith has made you well. Go in peace, and be healed of your affliction." (Mark 5:25-34)

This woman had this flow of blood for twelve years and had suffered many things from different doctors. She probably had been ridiculed and abused by those around her. But one day she heard about Jesus, and she decided to take her case to Him. She heard the Word, and she made a commitment to stop looking at her circumstance and start looking to Jesus Christ for the answer to her problems. In one single move, in one moment, her situation changed, and she was healed instantly. Your situation can change in one moment if you would turn it over to the Lord. Instead of focusing on your circumstance, begin to look to Jesus Christ; look to His Word and His promises for you. Then say to yourself, "I am taking this problem to Jesus and I believe He will turn it around. He will set me free if only I will call upon His name." Once you have made that confession to yourself, call on the name of Jesus and believe you are delivered. Ask Him to show you the way out of your predicament. He will do that for you. "For the Scripture says, *'Whoever believes on Him will not be put to shame.'* For *'whoever calls upon the name of the* Lord *shall be saved'*" (Romans 10:11,13).

SEE YOURSELF AS EQUAL TO OTHER PEOPLE

Equally important is how you see yourself in relation to other people. There are two opposite extremes of how people carry themselves in relation to other people. There are those who develop an inferiority complex when they stand before those whom they consider to be better than themselves, and there are those who may think they are superior to other people. Both of these attitudes are inappropriate; it is wrong to think one is inferior or superior to others.

Do you think you are inferior or superior to other people? Neither of these extreme complexes will help you if you truly want to walk in love. Part of loving yourself is to develop a balanced understanding of who you are in Christ Jesus. Don't think that you are less valuable or more valuable than others. We are all equal before God, and what happens to the poor man also happens to the rich man. What happens to those who are less fortunate in society will eventually happen to those who think they are smarter, sharper, more intelligent, stronger, more powerful, or richer.

> *Is it fitting* to say to a king, 'You are worthless,' And to nobles, '*You are* wicked'? Yet He is not partial to princes, nor does He regard the rich more than the poor; for they are all the work of His hands. (Job 34:18-19)

> The rich and the poor have this in common, the LORD *is* the maker of them all. (Proverbs 22:2)

> For *there is* no more remembrance of the wise than of the fool forever, since all that now *is* will be forgotten in the days to come. And how does a wise *man* die? As the fool! (Ecclesiastes 2:16)

HAVE THE RIGHT SELF-VALUE

Your self-value should grow from the inside to the outside and not the other way around. You cannot and should not value yourself on the basis of how you look or what you do on the outside. You are a spirit being, created in the image and likeness of God, and you have something greater and better on the inside than you have on the outside. You have more potential, more ability, and more beauty on the inside than is outwardly visible. God has placed something within you that is more valuable than anyone can comprehend by merely looking at your outward appearance. A word of caution, I am not saying you should neglect to take care of your body. I am not saying that your outward appearance is not important or that you should not exercise to keep fit and be in shape. What I am saying is that no matter how you look on the outside, you are very valuable to God.

> For You have formed my inward parts; You have covered me in my mother's womb. I will praise You, for I am fearfully *and* wonderfully made; marvelous are Your works, and *that* my soul knows very well. My frame was not hidden from You, when I was made in secret, *and* skillfully wrought in the lowest parts of the earth. Your eyes saw my substance, being yet unformed. And in Your book they all were written, the days fashioned for me, when as *yet there were* none of them. How precious also are Your thoughts to me, O God! How great is the sum of them! *If* I should count them, they would be more in number than the sand; When I awake, I am still with You. (Psalm 139:13-18)

Only God knows your true value because He is the one who formed you in your mother's womb. You were fearfully and wonderfully made by the Creator of the universe. He has placed something inside you that is greater than the world could imagine. You can discover your God-given value by spending time in His Word. Only the Word of God can tell you how much you are truly worth.

Don't Allow the World to Determine Your Worth

You should not take your value from the world. The world's value system is based only on what it can see, feel, or hear. The world tends to evaluate people on the basis of their material accomplishments rather than their true worth. The system is designed to destroy people's spiritual strength and make them slaves to the enemy of humankind, satan.

One problem with the world's value system is that in apportioning value to people, it usually matches one person's strength against another's weakness, then concludes that the latter is no good. But what the world fails to realize is that a person may appear weak physically but be very strong spiritually. Spiritual strength is far more important than physical strength. Another problem with the world's system is that its values are temporary; they don't last long. At the most, they last for a few years then depression and anxiety set in.

Unfortunately, many people have become slaves to the world's value system. There are many people in the world today who are in bondage to an unholy desire to be beautiful on the outside without caring about what is happening on the inside. Many times this is because society has given them the wrong impression that their self-worth comes from how beautiful they look. There is nothing wrong with being beautiful, but that is not your real value. Beauty may go away, but the real you will always remain. Who you are on the inside is more important than who you are on the outside. You are worth more than your outward beauty.

You are also worth more than what you have in the bank. Your money does not determine your self-worth. Jesus said, "For what profit is it to a man if he gains the whole world, and loses his own soul? Or what will a man give in exchange for his soul?" (Matthew 16:26). As a result of an incorrect value system, there are many in the world today who will do anything — good or bad — to increase financially without any qualms about what is happening to their spiritual lives. Many are willing to cling to political offices even if it means oppressing their fellow human beings.

Even our educational system is guilty of placing the wrong value on people. Their value is determined by education or the lack of it. No one has the right to say that a medical doctor is more valuable than a bus driver! No one has the right to say certain groups of students are better than other groups. The following true stories are perfect illustrations of how not to allow the world's educational system to be the judge of your value or your potential. They were taken from a book written by Steven K. Scott entitled, *Mentored by a Millionaire: Master Strategies of Super Achievers*.[1]

After graduating from high school at the bottom of his class, Michael L. did even worse in college. However, because he could throw a javelin farther than any other high school student in America, he landed a track scholarship to the University of Southern California. Unfortunately he flunked out his freshman year and ended up sleeping on park benches in Santa Monica. Even though Mike failed to achieve any success whatsoever in high school or college, he went on to become the most successful television actor, writer, and director in Hollywood history. Every single television series that he wrote, directed, or starred in became a huge prime time hit. No other actor, writer, or director has ever batted a thousand in television. How could someone who failed so miserably become so extraordinarily successful? And yet that is exactly what Michael Landon did.

Had Bill Lear not dropped out of school in the sixth grade, he would have read in the high school physics books of his day that it was impossible to make a radio small enough to fit into an automobile. Fortunately, he never read those books and went on to invent the first car radio. You could say that this was a fluke had he not also invented the autopilot, which radically changed the course of aviation. Later in his life, when the world's leading aviation companies said that there was no corporate market for small jets, and that building a prototype of such jet would cost more than $100 million, Bill created his prototype business jet for under $10 million and provided corporate aviation with affordable, practical, and reliable Lear Jets years before the aviation giants followed his lead.

And who would have given Tom E. even a prayer for success? After being pulled out of the first grade by his mother and being judged mentally retarded by the school's headmaster, Tom's business life didn't seem any more promising. Working for the railroad at the age of 12, he was fired after only a few months on the job. Yet this grade-school dropout not only invented the process of recording sound and making motion pictures, he gave us the first electric light bulb and over 1,000 other patented inventions. Even though he created more breakthrough inventions than any man in history, Thomas Edison would be the first to tell you that he was not a genius.

These stories prove that no one else can determine your potential. With God, you are capable of doing more than you can ever think or imagine. You are of God, and you can overcome whatever the enemy may throw at you. "You are of God, little children, and have overcome them, because He who is in you is greater than he who is in the world" (1 John 4:4).

The way to see your true value is to look through the eyes of God who created you and who knows you inside out. Only a biblical view of who you are in Christ Jesus can create in you a true and lasting appreciation of your potential and self-worth. You are very valuable in the eyes of God. As long as you maintain His viewpoint, the world's system cannot erase your self-value. The value He has placed on you is eternal. It is based on His Word and will remain long after the world's system has ceased to exist (Matthew 24:35; Mark 13:31; Luke 21:33).

TAKE YOUR VALUE FROM THE WORD OF GOD

Now let us look at your true value from the Word of God. These passages from both the Old and the New Testaments teach us about our true identity. Take time to meditate on them, confess them, and if possible, commit them to heart. These are only a few; there are many more in the Bible.

☞ *You are very valuable because you were created in the image of God.*[2]

> Then God said, "Let Us make man in Our image, according to Our likeness; let them have dominion over the fish of the sea, over the birds of the air, and over the cattle, over all the earth and over every creeping thing that creeps on the earth." So God created man in His *own* image; in the image of God He created him; male and female He created them. (Genesis 1:26-27)

In the very first chapter of the Bible, you can see that you are created in the image and likeness of God. You can have no higher value! In fact, you are the second most valuable entity in the whole universe! The only being that is of more value than you is God: Father, Son, and Holy Spirit. If you don't believe me, look at Psalm 8:3-8:

> When I consider Your heavens, the work of Your fingers, the moon and the stars, which You have ordained, what is man that You are mindful of him, and the son of man that You visit him? For You have made him a little lower than the angels, and You have crowned him with glory and honor. You have made him to have dominion over the works of Your hands; You have put all *things* under his feet, all sheep and oxen—even the beasts of the field, the birds of the air, and the fish of the sea that pass through the paths of the seas.

The word angels in the above scripture is the Hebrew word ELOHIM, which means God—we are created next in hierarchy to God. We are not equal to God or even near to Him in status, but God, in His infinite wisdom and love, chose to create us second in hierarchy to Himself.

👉 *You are valuable because you are a child of God.*[2]

> But as many as received Him, to them He gave the right to become children of God, to those who believe in His name: who were born, not of blood, nor of the will of the flesh, nor of the will of man, but of God. (John 1:12-13)

> Behold what manner of love the Father has bestowed on us, that we should be called children of God! Therefore the world does not know us, because it did not know Him. Beloved, now we are children of God; and it has not yet been revealed what we shall be, but we know that when He is revealed, we shall be like Him, for we shall see Him as He is. (1 John 3:1-2)

> For as many as are led by the Spirit of God, these are sons of God. For you did not receive the spirit of bondage again to fear, but you received the Spirit of adoption by whom we cry out, "Abba, Father." The Spirit Himself bears witness with our spirit that we are children of God, and if children, then heirs—heirs of God and joint heirs with Christ, if indeed we suffer with *Him*, that we may also be glorified together. (Romans 8:14-17)

Heir of God and joint heirs with Jesus Christ! We are born of God; therefore, we are children of God. There is no better, greater, more loving, or more caring father than the God who created the whole universe. Your biological parents may have abandoned you or abused you; society and the people around you may have forsaken you and turned their backs on you, but your heavenly Father is there for you. He cares for you very much, and His plan is to prosper you.

> For I know the thoughts that I think toward you, says the LORD, thoughts of peace and not of evil, to give you a future and a hope. (Jeremiah 29:11)

✎ *You are valuable because you are a new creature, created in Christ Jesus for good works.*[2]

> Therefore, if anyone *is* in Christ, *he is* a new creation; old things have passed away; behold, all things have become new. (2 Corinthians 5:17)

> For we are His workmanship, created in Christ Jesus for good works, which God prepared beforehand that we should walk in them. (Ephesians 2:10)

✎ *You are valuable because you are the righteousness of God through Christ Jesus.*[2]

> For He made Him who knew no sin *to be* sin for us, that we might become the righteousness of God in Him. (2 Corinthians 5:21)

✎ *You are valuable because you were redeemed at a very valuable price: the blood of Jesus Christ.*[2]

> Or do you not know that your body is the temple of the Holy Spirit *who is* in you, whom you have from God, and you are not your own? For you were bought at a price; therefore glorify God in your body and in your spirit, which are God's. (1 Corinthians 6:19-20)

> Knowing that you were not redeemed with corruptible things, *like* silver or gold, from your aimless conduct *received* by tradition from your fathers, but with the precious blood of Christ, as of a lamb without blemish and without spot. (1 Peter 1:18-19)

✎ *You are valuable because you are an instrument in God's hand to touch other people.*[2]

> Now all things are of God, who has reconciled us to Himself through Jesus Christ, and has given us the ministry of reconciliation, that is, that God was in

Christ reconciling the world to Himself, not imputing their trespasses to them, and has committed to us the word of reconciliation. Therefore we are ambassadors for Christ, as though God were pleading through us: we implore *you* on Christ's behalf, be reconciled to God. (2 Corinthians 5:18-20)

God has a plan and a purpose for all of us. You were not born for no reason. You were born for a purpose: God's purpose. You have a unique role to play in the work of the Kingdom. Only you can play that role, no one else can. You were born at the right time, at the right place, and for the right purpose. It is time for you to step into the plan and purpose God has for you. It may be that He wants you to help in full-time ministry, to help on a part-time basis, or to help finance the Gospel. There may be people only you can touch, and God is waiting for you to get with the program so He can use you to touch and change those people's lives. If you will ask Him, He will reveal His plan for you.

The following story is proof of what God can do through the hands of an ordinary person. It is the story of Benson A. Idahosa.[3] He was born in Benin City, Nigeria, to a poor pagan family. He was a very sickly child who was always fainting. Because of his constant illness, at the age of eighteen months, his father ordered Benson's mother to throw him into the dustbin outside hoping that he would die. However, Benson refused to die, but instead he started crying. The mother then retrieved him from the dustbin and raised him up all by herself. He had little or no education until he was about fourteen years old, when he started taking correspondence courses from Britain.

In spite of his precarious beginning, Archbishop Benson Andrew Idahosa (B. A. I.) later became an extremely influential minister of the Gospel. He was the founder and senior pastor of the Church of God Mission International, Inc., headquartered in Benin City, Nigeria. By 1981, he had established over 3,000 churches throughout Nigeria and Ghana, all within a period of ten years. He also built Benson Idahosa University, a christian university in Benin City, Nigeria. Today, the Church of God Mission International has planted churches in several other countries, including the United States and Japan.

If God can do it for Idahosa, He can do it for you, too. If you will trust God, cooperate with Him, and ask Him to show you His plan and purpose for your life, He will move you into your place of prosperity. God specializes in healing broken hearts and restoring people back to life. The God who created the universe, who empowered a ninety-year-old woman to give birth, who restored Job back to twice his former position, who enabled a virgin to give birth, and who raised Lazarus from the dead can restore you back to His glory.

Remember, God is not looking for those who can do the work; He is looking for those who will make themselves available for Him to use. He will equip you spiritually, intellectually, financially, or otherwise for whatever He has called you to do. Your responsibility is to follow Him, one step at a time. Nothing is too hard for the Lord. What is humanly impossible is possible with God. You are not the first person to be faced with difficult circumstances in life. There are many others before you who have faced insurmountable situations, whom the Lord has miraculously delivered. He has done it for billions of people before you. Since He created the universe, He has done nothing else but dig people out of their problems. I pray that what He did for others, He will do for you, in Jesus' name.

> Therefore Sarah laughed within herself, saying, "After I have grown old, shall I have pleasure, my lord being old also?" And the LORD said to Abraham, "Why did Sarah laugh, saying, 'Shall I surely bear *a child*, since I am old?' Is anything too hard for the LORD? At the appointed time I will return to you, according to the time of life, and Sarah shall have a son." (Genesis 18:12-14)

> Then the word of the LORD came to Jeremiah, saying, "Behold, I am the LORD, the God of all flesh. Is there anything too hard for Me?" (Jeremiah 32:26-27)

But Jesus looked at *them* and said to them, "With men this is impossible, but with God all things are possible." (Matthew 19:26)

"For with God nothing will be impossible." (Luke 1:37)

Jesus said to him, "If you can believe, all things *are* possible to him who believes." (Mark 9:23)

But He said, "The things which are impossible with men are possible with God." (Luke 18:27)

Chapter 10

Learn to Love Your Neighbor

The fourth step or dimension toward a fulfilled love life is to learn how to love your neighbor. Who is your neighbor? According to the Word of God, everyone qualifies: your spouse; your children (Ephesians 5:25, 33; Titus 2:4); other members of your household; your parents (Matthew 15:4); your siblings (1 John 2:10); fellow Christians (1 Peter 2:17; Ephesians 1:15); anyone who needs your help (Luke 10:29-37); colleagues; your enemies (Matthew 5:44); and all humans (1 Thessalonians 3:12-13).

The world is changing very rapidly; things are happening in quick succession, and Bible prophecies are being fulfilled every day. No doubt we are in the last days. Just as Jesus Christ prophesied, the world's economy is growing stronger by the day, and like in the days of Noah, and Sodom and Gomorrah, many people are eating, drinking, buying, selling, planting, and building more than ever before (Luke 17:26-28). The result is that people have little or no time for each other, and the love of many is growing cold.

However, as Christians we must not allow ourselves to be so busy that we neglect the most important thing in life: walking in love. We are under divine obligation to love our neighbors no matter what the rest of the world does.

Jesus answered him, "The first of all the commandments is: *'Hear, O Israel, the* LORD *our God, the* LORD *is one. And you shall love the* LORD *your God with all your heart, with all your soul, with all your mind, and with all your strength.'* This is the first commandment. And the second, like *it,* is this: *'You shall love your neighbor as yourself.'* There is no other commandment greater than these." (Mark 12:29-31)

Obviously it is very important that we learn how to love our neighbors. Fortunately, the Bible has given us some guidelines.

LOVE SACRIFICIALLY

We are to love one another as He, Jesus Christ gave command (1 John 3:23). "A new commandment I give to you, that you love one another; as I have loved you, that you also love one another" (John 13:34). Again in John 15:12, He said, "This is My commandment, that you love one another as I have loved you."

The question is how did He love us? "By this we know love, because He laid down His life for us. And we also ought to lay down *our* lives for the brethren" (1 John 3:16). In other words, God loved us by sacrificing Himself for our salvation. We needed a savior; God came down from Heaven in the person of Jesus Christ and paid the price for our salvation by dying on the cross for our sins.

Therefore, we are to love one another sacrificially. A sacrificial love will give all available resources to meet the needs of others. Sometimes we may have certain things we ordinarily would want to keep for ourselves, but this kind of love will compel us to use them for the benefit of other people. Real love is willing to give self and resources to serve others. This is more than loving in words; it is loving through actions. "But whoever has this world's goods, and sees his brother in need, and shuts up his heart from him, how does the love of God abide in him? My little children, let us not love in word or in tongue, but in deed and in truth" (1 John 3:17-18). So you see that if you have this world's goods (money, food, influence) and see someone in need and refuse to help such a person, the love of God is not in you. If you have the love of God, you will help those who are in need.

Some have said, "I thought I am supposed to love my neighbor as myself?" True! However, the New Testament commandment of love extends beyond that to include loving one another as we have been loved by Christ (John 13:34). As New Testament saints, we have something the Old Testament saints did not have. We have Christ as an example to follow. We also have the Holy Spirit living on the inside of us, and we can, by His power, love as Christ gave command. This was not the case with the Old Testament saints. They did not have the Holy Spirit living on the inside of them, and they did not have Jesus Christ as an example to follow. Therefore, they did not have the capacity to love as the Lord did.

We have the mind of Christ. He has demonstrated to us what real love is. We can love as Christ loved us because the love of God has been poured out in our hearts (Romans 5:5). In other words, we have the love of God, and we can actually love as Christ has loved us. We can do all things through Christ who strengthens us (Philippians 4:13).

That is not to say it is an easy thing to do. As a matter of fact, out of the five directional flows of love, this is the most difficult to achieve. Why? Because it involves someone else whose actions, more often than not, are outside of your control. As you walk in love you must remember that not everyone you seek to love will cooperate with you one hundred percent of the time. People are sometimes unpredictable. Some will stubbornly reject your good gestures, and some will even pay you back with evil. The key to all of these difficulties is to learn to exercise self-control so you do not become too assertive, need driven, or over-zealous. That is why it is vitally important to know the will of God in a situation before we step in to help. The willingness must be ours, but the plan must be God's.

No matter what others do, we are to love them as Christ has loved us. He clearly demonstrated His love toward us by taking our place when we were deserving of death and incapable of loving Him (Romans 5:8). In other words, He was selfless, forgiving, did not consider our sins, and willingly gave His very best to save us and reconcile us back to Himself. His decision was not based on who we were but on doing what God had already determined was right. When He was tempted to give in to pressure, He cried, "Not My will, Father, but let Your will be done."

In the same manner, we are required to love people unselfishly. We are to forgive and forget and not to consider other people's shortcomings in deciding whether to show them love. We are to love our enemies and those who despitefully use us. Jesus Christ summed it up this way:

> "You have heard that it was said, '*You shall love your neighbor* and hate your enemy.' But I say to you, love your enemies, bless those who curse you, do good to those who hate you, and pray for those who spitefully use you and persecute you, that you may be sons of your Father in heaven; for He makes His sun rise on the evil and on the good, and sends rain on the just and on the unjust. For if you love those who love you, what reward have you? Do not even the tax collectors do the same? And if you greet your brethren only, what do you do more *than* others? Do not even the tax collectors do so? Therefore you shall be perfect, just as your Father in heaven is perfect." (Matthew 5:43-48)

Love as a Servant

Another example of how Jesus Christ loved us is written in John 13:1-17. Verse 1 says that Jesus, "having loved His own who were in the world, He loved them to the end." The narrative then tells us how he demonstrated one aspect of this love. Jesus, fully aware of His authority as the Son of God, nevertheless, stooped down after supper, laid aside His garment, took a towel and a bowl of water, and began to wash the feet of His disciples. After which He spoke these words to them:

> "You call Me Teacher and Lord, and you say well, for *so* I am. If I then, *your* Lord and Teacher, have washed your feet, you also ought to wash one another's feet. For I have given you an example, that you should do as I have done to you. Most assuredly, I say to you, a servant is not greater than his master; nor is he who is sent greater than he who sent him. If you know these things, blessed are you if you do them." (John 13:13-17)

The example He gave is that we should be servant leaders. We should lay aside our pride and ego to serve others who need our help or service. In the Jewish custom, when the master of the house or a very important visitor comes in, a servant of the house takes a bowl of water and washes and dries their feet. Washing another person's feet usually signifies that the one who is washing the feet is the other's servant. The lesson from this passage is that willingness to serve is an act of love, and love will serve humbly without being proud.

It is very interesting that Jesus ended this line of discussion with the following statement, "If you know these things, blessed are you if you do them" (John 13:17). Which "things" is He referring to? He is referring to serving one another, and helping the poor and the weak among us. It is not enough to know it; you must do it.

Are you doing it? Are you helping those in need? Or are you offended at the sight of them? The blessing is not in the knowing. It is not in mentally agreeing to the idea. It is not what you know but what you actually do that counts. Jesus said,

> "Therefore whoever hears these sayings of Mine, and does them, I will liken him to a wise man who built his house on the rock: and the rain descended, the floods came, and the winds blew and beat on that house; and it did not fall, for it was founded on the

rock. Now everyone who hears these sayings of Mine, and does not do them, will be like a foolish man who built his house on the sand: and the rain descended, the floods came, and the winds blew and beat on that house; and it fell. And great was its fall."
(Matthew 7:24-27)

The best love is that shown to someone who is less fortunate than you and who probably can never repay you. Those who are rich in the society must reach out and help those who are poor. The powerful should take the initiative to help the weak among them. Do not wait for the weak to come to you; go after them and help them as much as you can. As you help the weak, the Lord will add more resources to you. Imagine what would have happened if God had waited for us to come to Him. He did not wait for us; He came down to seek us out by Himself.

Sometimes we are so focused on loving those around us that we lose track of the fact that there are other people out there who need our love too. Or we may be so focused on not getting enough love from those around us that we lose sight of the fact that there are many out there that we should love. Those who seek to love other people will never go unloved. Those who endeavor to help others will always be helped. If you are looking for love, step out to love those who are in more difficult situations than yours, and you will find more love than you thought possible. It is called the law of sowing and reaping: You will reap whatever you sow.

Learn to Love Your Enemies

To love your neighbors includes loving your enemies. There is no better way to demonstrate the God-kind of love than to love our enemies. This is the ultimate test of real love. It is easy to love those who are good to you, but what about those who have offended you and have done you harm? There is always the temptation to strike back in retaliation when someone does something bad to you.

This is one of the most important themes of Jesus' ministry. Most of the time, Jesus' teachings center on loving the enemy, the sinner, the sick, the poor, the oppressed, and other less fortunate ones in society. Jesus' teaching in Matthew 5:44 to "Love your enemies, bless those who curse you, do good to those who hate you, and pray for those who spitefully use you and persecute you," is a radical departure from what the Jews had been taught in the Old Testament. In the Old Testament, the Jews were taught to love their neighbor (those who love them) and hate their enemies. They were taught to practice the law of retaliation.

The name of the game was life for life, eye for eye, tooth for tooth, hand for hand, foot for foot, burning for burning, wound for wound, and stripe for stripe (Exodus 21:23-25). Under the law, the injured parties were permitted to avenge themselves upon the ones who inflicted the injury. Under that same law, if your heart was broken by someone committing adultery with your spouse, he or she was to be stoned to death.

The reason for this is because the Old Testament saints were not born again. They did not have the Spirit of God living on the inside of them. They may have been anointed by the Holy Spirit to do certain work, but their spirits were not alive to God. Salvation—spiritual rebirth—came by Jesus Christ. No one in the Old Testament was born again. In the Old Testament, we are told that, "The heart is deceitful above all things, and desperately wicked; who can know it?" (Jeremiah 17:9). This scripture refers to the heart of a sinful person before regeneration. At regeneration—that is the new birth—when a person accepts Jesus Christ as Lord, he or she receives a new heart and become a new person.

At regeneration, God sprinkles us with the blood of His begotten Son, Jesus Christ. We are cleansed from our filthiness and from idols. He gives us a new heart, a heart of flesh, a new spirit. He takes away the old, stony, and wicked heart and places His Spirit in us. By His Spirit, we can now walk in His statutes and obey His commandments. It is written that "if anyone *is* in Christ, *he is* a new creature; old things have passed away; behold, all things have become new" (2 Corinthians 5:17).

Unlike the Old Testament saints, the love of God has been shed abroad in our hearts by the Holy Spirit, which was given to us (Romans 5:5). God has given us His Spirit, His love, His grace, His enablement to do what the Old Testament saints could not do. We now have the capacity, and we can love our enemies, even as Christ has loved us.

How to Love Your Enemies

Bless Your Enemies

One way to love your enemies is to bless them. Jesus said, we should bless them that curse us (Matthew 5:44). The word "bless" comes from the Greek word *Eulogeo*, meaning to cause to prosper, to make happy, and to bestow the favor of God upon someone.[1] In other words, we are to help our enemies to prosper in whatever they are doing. Note that you do not wait for them to repent or ask for your forgiveness before you bless them. You bless them even while they are still cursing, hating, or persecuting you.

> For when we were still without strength, in due time Christ died for the ungodly. For scarcely for a righteous man will one die; yet perhaps for a good man someone would even dare to die. But God demonstrates His own love toward us, in that while we were still sinners, Christ died for us. (Romans 5:6-8)

God did not wait for the world to repent before He began to pour out His blessing upon us. His blessing is already there for us to tap into at anytime we choose to accept His work of salvation. God gave His Son even while we were yet in sin. He predestined the human race for salvation even before the foundation of the world. He also blessed us with every spiritual blessing in heavenly places even before we repented and accepted Jesus Christ as Lord.

> Blessed be the God and Father of our Lord Jesus Christ, who has blessed us with every spiritual blessing in the heavenly *places* in Christ, just as He chose us in Him before the foundation of the world, that we should be holy and without blame before Him in love, having predestined us to adoption as sons by Jesus Christ to Himself, according to the good pleasure of His will. (Ephesians 1:3-5)

Do Good to Your Enemies

Another way to love your enemies is to do good to them. When someone acts wickedly or offensively towards you, look for an opportunity to show them some kindness. Find out what they need, ask the Lord to show you how to meet that need, then act on what He shows you. As we saw previously, knowledge is not enough; actions are needed.

> Repay no one evil for evil. Have regard for good things in the sight of all men. If it is possible, as much as depends on you, live peaceably with all men. Beloved, do not avenge yourselves, but *rather* give place to wrath; for it is written, *"Vengeance is Mine, I will repay,"* says the Lord. Therefore *"if your enemy is hungry, feed him; if he is thirsty, give him a drink; for in so doing you will heap coals of fire on his head."* Do not be overcome by evil, but overcome evil with good. (Romans 12:17-21)

Share the good things you have with your enemy. Buy some very special presents to show them you care. Where possible and expedient, buy them food when they are hungry, or take them for a very special outing. Invite them to your home, if expedient, and feed them graciously and cheerfully. Do these things in love and sincerity, not so that you entice them to love or appreciate you but to show them you truly care for them. For God makes His sun to shine on the evil as well as on the good. He makes His rain to fall on the just as well as the unjust (Matthew 5:45). In other words, when God rains down His blessings, He does not discriminate.

When it became necessary that the Word of God be placed in the hands of all, God inspired men to invent the printing press for the printing of the Bible. Today the printing press is available to all, without any exception. When it became necessary to take the Gospel to the rest of the world, God inspired men to invent the airplane and other media to quickly dispense the Word. Today the airplane and multimedia are readily available to anyone who wishes to use them. When God's people cried for divine healing, God anointed His servants with the healing anointing and inspired doctors and scientists to discover cures for various ailments. Toda, all of these cures and medical breakthroughs and abilities are available to everyone.

And when our fallen state cried out for a savior, Jesus Christ died for the world. "For God so loved the world that He gave His only begotten Son, that whoever believes in Him should not perish but have everlasting life" (John 3:16). Today, salvation is available to everyone who requests it—no exceptions.

PRAY FOR YOUR ENEMIES

Another way to love your enemies is to pray for them. Jesus is a perfect example of this. At the Cross of Calvary, even though He was in agonizing pain, He looked down on those who were crucifying Him and at the elders and priests who delivered Him up to be crucified and prayed, "Father, forgive them, for they do not know what they do" (Luke 23:34).

Another perfect example was Stephen, one of the seven deacons chosen by the Apostles to help care for the widows of the first Christian church at Jerusalem (Acts 6:1-7). He was described as a man full of faith and power, who did great wonders and miracles among the people (Acts 6:8). He also spoke with wisdom and in the Spirit, and as a result, the Jewish religious leaders accused him falsely, and after a mock trial, he was sentenced to death by stoning.

The scripture says Stephen was led out of the city and stoned. As they were stoning him, he knelt down and prayed for his attackers:

> Then they cried out with a loud voice, stopped their ears, and ran at him with one accord; and they cast *him* out of the city and stoned *him*. And the witnesses laid down their clothes at the feet of a young man named Saul. And they stoned Stephen as he was calling on *God* and saying, "Lord Jesus, receive my spirit." Then he knelt down and cried out with a loud voice, "Lord, do not charge them with this sin." And when he had said this, he fell asleep. (Acts 7:57-60)

We should all learn to pray for our enemies. It is not only godly, it brings blessing.

> Finally, all of *you be* of one mind, having compassion for one another; love as brothers, be tenderhearted, be courteous; not returning evil for evil or reviling for reviling, but on the contrary blessing, knowing that you were called to this, that you may inherit a blessing. (1 Peter 3:8-9)

Loving Your Neighbor: Not As Difficult as You Think

To love our neighbor as Christ has loved us is not as difficult as we think, if only we will look at it in context of the scripture.

1 *Real love does not require more than we have or are able to give.* Jesus did not give us more than Himself. He gave us all that was required and all that was within His power to give. No more and no less. We must always ask these questions: What does real love require of me in this circumstance? Do I have the resources or the capacity to provide the required solution to this person's problem? What can I do to help, even if I cannot meet the entire need? Sometimes all real love requires may be a prayer, a hearing ear, counsel, or a kind word.

2 *Sacrificial love must be seen within the confines of the characteristics of real love.* (See Chapter 3.) Memorize the characteristics of love and apply them in your relationships. Practice them in your home, work place, church, and other places you may find yourself. When a situation arises, learn to speak the things real love requires in that particular situation. Comfort yourself, counsel yourself, and talk to yourself. "Love suffers long, so I will suffer long in this situation." "Love forgives, so I will forgive that person."

Chapter 11
Learn to Receive Love from Other People

The fifth dimension of real love is to learn to receive love from other people. This requires that you learn both how to receive other people's love as well as how to respond when they don't love you. We all have a desire to be loved by those with whom we come in contact in our daily lives. We want them to give us affirmation, affection, sympathy, encouragement, and support. The bad news is that this desire to be loved is the most elusive aspect of the five dimensions of love. For most people, it is almost non-existent, and where it exists, it is usually short-lived. Sooner or later it leads to doubtfulness, frustration, disappointment, anger, and resentfulness.[1]

There are several reasons why our desire to be loved by others may never be fulfilled, at least not to the extent we desire. Jesus said that in the last days "because lawlessness will abound, the love of many will grow cold" (Matthew 24:12). We seem to be living in that day. People now place more value on material things than they do on people. Husbands and wives are more interested in their careers and the pursuit of wealth than they are in their families. As a result, parents are no longer as committed to the future of their children as they once were.

The down side of our strong economy is that people are working longer hours with little or no time to build love relationships. There is always something new to spend money on, so they work more hours to make more money, so they can buy more things, so they can measure up to their peers. Even though the economy is growing stronger, more and more people are getting into more and more debt. Someone who has a bundle of debt hanging over his or her head cannot give or receive much love because the pressure of trying to pay it off is too great. Where relationships do exist, they have too often become an avenue to offload on people rather than a desire to love. People get into relationships with the mindset of seeking an opportunity to make a profit out of every friendly discussion. Networking for profit has become the order of the day.

Another reason for the elusiveness of love from others is the fact that there are so many misconceptions concerning love. If a person is not born again, or if they have not come to an understanding of God's love for them, their concept of love is at variance with His. As a result, they hardly recognize the God-kind of love, even if it is staring at them in the face. In other words, there is a mismatch between what people are looking for and what real love is. The desire for love is created by God, who Himself is love. If someone is looking for a love that differs from that which God placed within us, there will be a mismatch, and the result will be frustration, bitterness, and pain. On the other hand, if you know what you truly need, you can easily identify it when you see it, and you will be satisfied. For example, if your idea of love is that people will overlook all of your errors without attempting to correct you, then your definition of love is at variance with God's definition of real love. As a result, you will always feel dissatisfied with the love you are getting from other people, because each time you are corrected you will be offended.

However, the most important reason why other people's love is hard to find is because we are looking for the right thing in the wrong places. As part of my preparation to write this book, I searched the Bible for instances where the Word instructs us to expect love from other people. To my great surprise, there appears to be none. Nowhere in the Bible did God specifically ask us to look up to other people for love. As a matter of fact, it appears that to have an insatiable desire for people's love is a curse. I am not saying you are cursed if you desire love from others. What I am saying is that if you have an insatiable desire for their love and approval you are operating as if you are still under the curse. No Christian should operate under the curse.

> To the woman He said: "I will greatly multiply your sorrow and your conception; in pain you shall bring forth children; your desire *shall be* for your husband, and he shall rule over you." Then to Adam He said, "Because you have heeded the voice of your wife, and have eaten from the tree of which I commanded you, saying, 'You shall not eat of it': Cursed *is* the ground for your sake; in toil you shall eat *of* it all the days of your life. Both thorns and thistles it shall bring forth for you, and you shall eat the herb of the field. In the sweat of your face you shall eat bread till you return to the ground, for out of it you were taken; for dust you *are*, and to dust you shall return." (Genesis 3:16-19)

The good news is that we do not have to operate under that curse any more because we have been redeemed.

> Christ has redeemed us from the curse of the law, having become a curse for us (for it is written, *"Cursed is everyone who hangs on a tree"*), that the blessing of Abraham might come upon the Gentiles in Christ Jesus, that we might receive the promise of the Spirit through faith. (Galatians 3:13-14)

Just as we seek to overcome the curses listed in Genesis 3:17-19 (poverty), we should also seek to overcome the curse listed in Genesis 3:16 (unholy desire for other people's love or acceptance).

Receiving Love from Unbelievers

We must understand that there are two classes of people on the earth: believers and unbelievers. I have come to understand that as a believer, I cannot expect an unbeliever to show me the God-kind of love. The reason for this is because unbelievers lack the ability to walk in real love. They cannot love you as Christ loves you, and they cannot even love you as they love themselves because Christ is not in them.

How can unbelievers love you as Christ loves you when they do not believe in Him? Jesus said if they love Him they will love you, and if they hate Him they will hate you, too (John 15:18-20). He also said, "He who does not love Me does not keep My words; and the word which you hear is not Mine but the Father's who sent Me" (John 14:24). Unbelievers have not yet learned how to love Jesus Christ; so, you cannot expect them to keep His commandment of love.

In the Old Testament, the commandment to love your neighbor as yourself was given to God's people, the Israelites; it was not given to the nations around them. In the New Testament, the commandment to love one another was given to the Church and not to the unbeliever. Therefore, we cannot expect unbelievers to give us real love, and we must not demand it from them.

However, unbelievers can sometimes demonstrate a semblance of love. Nevertheless, these demonstrations are conditional rather than real love. They are based on certain conditions. They are not the God-kind of love that is unconditional. As long as you meet those conditions, they will continue to show love, but when you step out of their expectations, the love is withdrawn.

The mere fact that unbelievers can demonstrate a semblance of real love is not sufficient reason for us to demand that they walk in it. To do so would be to place a burden on them which they are unable to bear. If we want them to walk in real love, we must first seek to get them saved. Only those who are saved have the love of God shed abroad in their hearts. When an unbeliever shows any form of love, we should see it as an honor. We should appreciate it and let them know how much it means to us. We should then use it as an opportunity to witness the truth of the Gospel to them.

Receiving Love from Believers

What about believers? Believers are under obligation to love as Christ loves. However, the obligation is not to you but to God. Spiritually speaking, we are not responsible to any person to keep the commandment. Our responsibility is to God. "Who are you to judge another's servant? To his own master he stands or falls. Indeed, he will be made to stand, for God is able to make him stand" (Romans 14:4).

We expect believers to love us as Christ loves us because God commands them to do so. However, we cannot *demand* that they love us. It is counterproductive to attempt to put pressure on other people to love you. The more pressure you apply, the more difficult you are to love. It is much better for them to love you out of their own free will and not out of compulsion. Focus on showing love. What you sow, you will reap.

It would be wise for married couples to keep this in mind. Marriages are put under tremendous stress when one of the couple, or both, are putting pressure on the other to show them more love. Sometimes people want to replace God's love with human love. As we've already discussed, that does not work.

No person can give you what only God can give. True and lasting satisfaction in life comes only from God. You will have fulfillment if—and only if—you look to God for all you need instead of looking to people for satisfaction, even if the other person happens to be your spouse. It is written, "Thus says the Lord: "Cursed *is* the man who trusts in man and makes flesh his strength, whose heart departs from the Lord" (Jeremiah 17:5). It is better to trust in the Lord than to put your confidence in humans. Does that mean we should not desire to be loved? No it does not. God gave us that desire, so we do desire to be loved, but we must make sure that desire does not become misdirected.

DEVELOP THE RIGHT ATTITUDE

To experience other people's love, we must develop a right concept of love. We must also show ourselves friendly (Proverbs 18:24). We must have the right character and attitude toward life. Wrong character and attitude toward life will rob us of good friends. However, no matter how hard we have worked at perfecting our attitude and character, we should not expect perfect love from others. As a matter of fact, we should endeavor to give to others all the love that we can, receive all the love God has offered us, and expect none from others. In other words, turn to God for all our need for love, and consider any love we receive from others as a bonus.

I personally believe that if we do not look to others for love, we will not be disappointed or hurt if they give us none. That does not mean we do not take it if we find it, but it does mean we do not expect too much from other people. The good news is that if we are walking in real love, love will find us because first of all, we will be easy to love; and secondly, we reap whatever we sow.

Chapter 12
The Ultimate Solution

The ultimate solution to the problem of giving and receiving real love is the Word of God. Real love comes from the heart. It is an issue of the heart and not an issue of the mind or the intellect. There is no formula outside of the Word of God that will produce real changes in your heart, which is what you need if you truly desire to walk in love.

Walking in love is not transferable, and it cannot be imparted. Outside the Word of God, there is no prescription or formula that will fit everyone. Our experiences and capacities both to give and to receive are different. The people you deal with are different from those with whom I deal. Before we seek to apply the various strategies on how to love, we must first develop a natural disposition to want to walk in love. When something in you is naturally disposed to walk in real love, then it becomes much easier to apply the different principles. The body must first be trained to want to do right before it is taught how to do right.

Love is not something we learn to do; it is something we become. It is something that begins on the inside and manifests itself on the outside. To experience real love, a fundamental change must occur on the inside of you. The nature of love must not only be sown in your heart, it must be developed until it flows out of you naturally, without any hindrance. Only

God can bring about such a change, and He does it through His Word.

Love is a spiritual force. Like all spiritual forces, it comes from the Word of God. Jesus said, "It is the Spirit who gives life; the flesh profits nothing. The words that I speak to you are spirit, and *they* are life" (John 6:63). God's Word is Spirit, and it has the power to transform you. It does not matter how bad you may have been in the past, when you begin to expose yourself to the Word, it will change you from the inside to the outside.

I once was a skeptic of the Bible. I used to see it as another book written by very brilliant men until I got saved. Now I can defend the power of the Word of God with my life. What brought about those changes? It was exposure to the Word. As I began to expose myself to the Word, it began to change me inside out. By virtue of the society in which I was born, I grew up with very little to no understanding about what it meant to walk in love. As far as love was concerned, I was a complete novice. I was born in a city where people take offending other people for granted and where fighting each other is very commonplace. The good news is that all of that has changed within me. I have become more meek and humble than I used to be. Presently, I seek to walk in love daily. What brought the changes? It is the infallible Word of God. Through the Word, I have been cultivating a nature of real love from the inside, which is now easily manifested in my outward dealings with other people.

My first few weeks of marriage were tough. I was always insisting that things be done my way and my way alone. I was almost a controlling machine. At a point, I knew I was too hard on my wife, and that some of the things I did and said were wrong, but I did not know how to stop. As I prayed over the situation, it suddenly occurred to me that the solution to my problem was in the Word of God. That was when I started spending time with God, especially searching out those scriptures that deal with love. The more time I spent reading the love scriptures, which I have put together in this book, the more I began to change. My character and attitude towards my wife and toward other people began to change for the better. To God's glory, I can confidently say that the Word has changed me dramatically, and I am miles away from where I started. God's Words on love have literally changed my character and temperament. Like the Apostle Paul, I do not count myself to be perfect yet, but one thing I know is that I am pressing forward towards perfection (Philippians 3:13). That is my ultimate goal. My desire is to take you along with me. If you will diligently apply the various scriptures quoted in this book, you will be amazed by what they will do for your walk of love.

The Word is a transformer. It is also a healer. It can heal all kinds of sickness, disease, and pain. It can heal all kinds of emotional problems: anger, impatience, insecurity, unforgiveness, insensitivity, and other issues that are road blocks to walking in love. It will heal everything that needs healing. It will remove impediments, restore joy, rebuild and heal broken hearts, and motivate discouraged spirits.

God created the universe, including humanity, with His words.

> In the beginning was the Word, and the Word was with God, and the Word was God. He was in the beginning with God. All things were made through Him, and without Him nothing was made that was made. (John 1:1-3)

Everything God does in this world, He does it through the words of His mouth. He said, "Let there be light," and light was (Genesis 1:3). "Let Us make man in our own image," and man was created in the image of God (Genesis 1:26-27). He spoke to a virgin, Mary, through the mouth of an angel, Gabriel, and she conceived and gave birth to a son, Jesus (Luke 1:26-38; 2:7). We were saved by the power of God's Holy Spirit, by grace through faith in His Word (Romans 10:8-13).

Like salvation, we develop the God-kind of love by reading the Word, meditating on it, and confessing it with our mouth.

When you read the Word and meditate on it, it changes you from the inside. When you put that Word in your mouth and begin to confess it, it releases spiritual powers that transform your life until you become what you have read and confessed over and over again. Abraham understood this principle when he began to call himself the father of many nations. David understood this principle, and he used it over and over again in the Psalms. Paul applied these principles when he said repeatedly, "I am the righteousness of God in Christ Jesus." Jesus Christ said repeatedly, "as the Father has told me, so I speak."

Jesus, after commanding the disciples to walk in love, prayed for them. One of the prayers He prayed was, "Sanctify them by Your truth. Your word is truth" (John 17:17). One of the meanings of the word sanctify is to purify internally, to cleanse, and to set apart unto God. The word has the power to set you apart unto love. Remember God is love. If you are set apart unto God, you are set apart unto love. If you are in the presence of Love, you will do love, speak love, and receive love. It is as simple as that.

It is time for you to speak what the Bible says about your love life. It is time to fill your heart with the Word of God on love and start confessing that you are love because you are a child of God, who is love. Jesus, in the Sermon on the Mount says, "Therefore you shall be perfect, just as your Father in heaven is perfect" (Matthew 5:48).

I challenge you to diligently study and meditate on the following love scriptures and regularly recite the love confessions. Together they will change your life forever. I am speaking from experience. Your love life will improve more than a hundred fold. Read the Word of God, meditate on it, confess it, and watch it change you from the inside until you naturally respond in love no matter what the circumstances are.

"For My thoughts *are* not your thoughts, Nor *are* your ways My ways," says the LORD. "For *as* the heavens are higher than the earth, so are My ways higher than your ways, and My thoughts than your thoughts. For as the rain comes down, and the snow from heaven, and do not return there, but water the earth, and make it bring forth and bud, that it may give seed to the sower and bread to the eater, so shall My word be that goes forth from My mouth; It shall not return to Me void, but it shall accomplish what I please, and it shall prosper *in the thing* for which I sent it." (Isaiah 55:8-11)

May the Word of God that you read prosper and change you inside out until you are a perfect reflection of Jesus Christ. As you sow these words in your heart, I pray that they will bear much fruit. Get ready. You are about to experience a tremendous change in your life, in your relationships, and in your walk with God. May God visit you in your home with His supernatural blessing; may He enlarge your territory and prosper your spirit, soul, and body, in Jesus' name I pray, Amen.

Love Scriptures

These scriptures are divided into five groups. The first group of scriptures will help you appreciate and believe the love that God has for you. The second group will help you develop real love for God. The third group will help you develop real love for yourself. The fourth group will help you develop real love for your neighbor. The fifth group will help you appreciate other people's love for you. All of these scriptures are designed to build within you a supernatural love for God and for others. Carefully meditate on them, and note the things the Word has to say about God's love, your love, and other people's love. Then speak out the confessions that follow. All of these scriptures apply to you as much as to any person that will put them to work. They are timeless, infallible truths that you can rely on, and they will work for you if you will put them to work. Read them and confess them over and over again until you begin to see yourself walk naturally in love.

Group 1
Scriptures to Help You Receive God's Love

🔖 *You are created in the Image and Likeness of God.*

Then God said, "Let Us make man in Our image, according to Our likeness; let them have dominion over the fish of the sea, over the birds of the air, and over the cattle, over all the earth and over every creeping thing that creeps on the earth." So God created man in His *own* image; in the image of God He created him; male and female He created them. Then God blessed them, and God said to them, "Be fruitful and multiply; fill the earth and subdue it; have dominion over the fish of the sea, over the birds of the air, and over every living thing that moves on the earth." (Genesis 1:26-28)

Confession

I am created in the image and likeness of God. I know that God loves me because I am created in His own image and likeness. God has given me dominion over all that He created. I have dominion over everything that swims in the sea, over everything that flies in the air, over every animal in the field, over all that creeps and grows on the earth, and over all other resources of the earth. He has commanded me to be fruitful and to multiply; I will be fruitful, and I will multiply in Jesus' name.

🔖 *You are created a little Lower than Elohim.*

When I consider Your heavens, the work of Your fingers, the moon and the stars, which You have ordained, what is man that You are mindful of him, and the son of man that You visit him? For You have made him a little lower than the angels, and You have crowned him with glory and honor. You have made him to have dominion over the works of Your hands; You have put all *things* under his feet. (Psalm 8:3-6)

CONFESSION

I am created a little lower than God. After God (Father, Son and Holy Spirit), I am the most important being on the face of the universe. God is very mindful of me. He loves me so much He gave His only begotten Son, Jesus, to die for my sins. I am not a "nobody." Jesus did not die for a nobody. I am special, that is why He died to set me free.

God's love for you is everlasting.

The LORD has appeared of old to me, *saying*: "Yes, I have loved you with an everlasting love; therefore with lovingkindness I have drawn you." (Jeremiah 31:3)

Sing, O heavens! Be joyful, O earth! And break out in singing, O mountains! For the LORD has comforted His people, and will have mercy on His afflicted. But Zion said, "The LORD has forsaken me, and my Lord has forgotten me." "Can a woman forget her nursing child, and not have compassion on the son of her womb? Surely they may forget, yet I will not forget you. See, I have inscribed you on the palms *of My hands*; your walls are continually before Me." (Isaiah 49:13-16)

God's love for you is everlasting. His mercy endures forever, and His faithfulness is forevermore. God's love is not momentary; it is neither short-term nor long-term. It is eternal, forever and ever. It is not conditional, and it will never die or fade away. No matter what sin you may have committed, God still loves you. When you sin, quickly confess your sins, and

He is faithful and just to forgive your sins and to cleanse you of all unrighteousness. God's love for you knows no bound. It never changes; it is the same yesterday, today, and forever. You are engraved in the palm of God's hand, and no one can take you from Him. Jesus says,

> "My sheep hear My voice, and I know them, and they follow Me. And I give them eternal life, and they shall never perish; neither shall anyone snatch them out of My hand. My Father, who has given *them* to Me, is greater than all; and no one is able to snatch *them* out of My Father's hand." (John 10:27-29)

As long as you continue to confess Jesus Christ as your Lord, you will forever remain a child of God, and you will continually be before Him. God has not forsaken you; the Lord has not forgotten you. Just as a woman cannot forget her nursing child, God cannot forget you. His love for you is everlasting.

CONFESSION

God's love for me is everlasting. He will never leave me nor forsake me. Therefore, I will sing for joy; I will rejoice with gladness of heart because the Lord comforts me and has had mercy on me. God will not forget me but will have compassion on me. I am inscribed in the palm of God's hand, and my face is continually before Him. Jesus Christ has given me eternal life, and I hear His voice always. Therefore, no one can snatch me out of His hand nor can they separate me from His love.

☙ **God demonstrated His love for us by sacrificing His own Son, Jesus Christ, for our sins.**

"For God so loved the world that He gave His only begotten Son, that whoever believes in Him should not perish but have everlasting life." (John 3:16)

> But God demonstrates His own love toward us, in that while we were still sinners, Christ died for us. (Romans 5:8)
>
> In this the love of God was manifested toward us, that God has sent His only begotten Son into the world, that we might live through Him. (1 John 4:9)
>
> But God, who is rich in mercy, because of His great love with which He loved us, even when we were dead in trespasses, made us alive together with Christ (by grace you have been saved), and raised *us* up together, and made *us* sit together in the heavenly *places* in Christ Jesus, that in the ages to come He might show the exceeding riches of His grace in *His* kindness toward us in Christ Jesus. (Ephesians 2:4-7)

God's love for us remains the same, regardless of the sins we may have committed. He has always loved us, still loves us, and will always love us for eternity to come. Nothing shall be able to separate us from the love of God. No sin and no individual is powerful enough to separate us from the love of God. It is vitally important that you believe this and claim it for yourself and your loved ones. Scripture teaches that if we sin against God, we should confess our sins and "He is faithful and just to forgive us *our* sins and to cleanse us from all unrighteousness" (1 John 1:9).

CONFESSION

God demonstrated His love for me by sending His only begotten Son, Jesus Christ, to die on the Cross for my sins. I believe that Jesus is the Son of God; I believe that He died on the Cross for me; I believe that He rose again from the dead; I believe that because He lives I too will live forever in Heaven with Him. I confess that Jesus is Lord. He is my Lord; He is my Savior; He is my Redeemer forever.

❦ *Jesus' death and resurrection is a perfect seal of God's love for humanity.*

What then shall we say to these things? If God *is* for us, who *can be* against us? He who did not spare His own Son, but delivered Him up for us all, how shall He not with Him also freely give us all things? (Romans 8:31-32)

Who shall bring a charge against God's elect? *It is* God who justifies. Who is he who condemns? *It is* Christ who died, and furthermore is also risen, who is even at the right hand of God, who also makes intercession for us. (Romans 8:33-34)

Who shall separate us from the love of Christ? *Shall tribulation, or distress, or persecution, or famine, or nakedness, or peril, or sword? As it is written: "For Your sake we are killed all day long; we are accounted as sheep for the slaughter."* Yet in all these things we are more than conquerors through Him who loved us. (Romans 8:35-37)

For I am persuaded that neither death nor life, nor angels nor principalities nor powers, nor things present nor things to come, nor height nor depth, nor any other created thing, shall be able to separate us from the love of God which is in Christ Jesus our Lord. (Romans 8:38-39)

I have been crucified with Christ; it is no longer I who live, but Christ lives in me; and the *life* which I now live in the flesh I live by faith in the Son of God, who loved me and gave Himself for me. (Galatians 2:20)

And from Jesus Christ, the faithful witness, the firstborn from the dead, and the ruler over the kings of the earth. To Him who loved us and washed us from our sins in His own blood. (Revelation 1:5)

CONFESSION

God is for me, therefore no person or being can stand against me. He, who did not spare His own Son for me, will always protect me and freely give me everything that pertains to life. Nothing shall be able to separate me from the love of God. I have been crucified with Christ; it is no longer I who live, but Christ lives in me; and the life, which I now live in the flesh, I live by faith in the Son of God, who loved me and gave Himself for me. Therefore, I am more than a conqueror through Him who loved me.

God's love is bestowed love.

"For the Father Himself loves you, because you have loved Me, and have believed that I came forth from God." (John 16:27)

Behold what manner of love the Father has bestowed on us, that we should be called children of God! (1 John 3:1)

And we have known and believed the love that God has for us. God is love, and he who abides in love abides in God, and God in him. (1 John 4:16)

God's love for humans is bestowed love. It is a free gift, an honor bestowed on humanity. It has nothing to do with what we did or did not do; rather, it has everything to do with who God is. He chose to create us and to love us with an everlasting love. It was a deliberate choice, and He is faithful to keep loving us to the end.

CONFESSION

God's love for me is an unconditional love. His love for me has nothing to do with my good works or lack of them. Whatever I receive from God is a free gift from Him. He blesses me everyday because He loves me and not because of what I do or not do. God is love, and I will abide in Him forever.

❦ *God is longsuffering, merciful, and full of compassion.*

But You, O Lord, *are* a God full of compassion, and gracious, longsuffering and abundant in mercy and truth. (Psalm 86:15)

He will again have compassion on us, and will subdue our iniquities. You will cast all our sins into the depths of the sea. (Micah 7:19)

If You, LORD, should mark iniquities, O Lord, who could stand? But *there is* forgiveness with You, that You may be feared. (Psalm 130:3-4)

"But if a wicked man turns from all his sins which he has committed, keeps all My statutes, and does what is lawful and right, he shall surely live; he shall not die. None of the transgressions which he has committed shall be remembered against him; because of the righteousness which he has done, he shall live. Do I have any pleasure at all that the wicked should die?" says the Lord GOD, "and not that he should turn from his ways and live?" (Ezekiel 18:21-23)

In Him we have redemption through His blood, the forgiveness of sins, according to the riches of His grace. (Ephesians 1:7)

If we confess our sins, He is faithful and just to forgive us *our* sins and to cleanse us from all unrighteousness. (1 John 1:9)

Bless the LORD, O my soul; and all that is within me, *bless* His holy name! Bless the LORD, O my soul, and forget not all His benefits: Who forgives all your iniquities, who heals all your diseases, who redeems your life from destruction, who crowns you with lovingkindness and tender mercies, who satisfies your mouth with good things, *so that your* youth is renewed like the eagle's. (Psalm 103:1-5)

God's love is demonstrated in His patience, mercy, and compassion. God is gracious, longsuffering, and abounds in mercy. He is slow to anger and to judge.

Confession

I bless You, O Lord, with my soul; and with all that is within me, I bless Your holy name! I will not forget all of Your benefits. You forgive all my iniquities, You heal all my diseases, You redeem my life from destruction, You crown me with lovingkindness and tender mercies, You satisfy my mouth with good things so that my youth is renewed like the eagle's.

You, O Lord, are a God full of compassion, graciousness, longsuffering, and abundant in mercy and truth. You have cast all my sins into the depths of the sea; I am no longer a sinner. I have redemption through the blood of Your Son, Jesus Christ. As I confess my sins, You are faithful and just to forgive me my sins and to cleanse me from all unrighteousness.

GROUP 2
SCRIPTURES TO HELP YOU CULTIVATE LOVE FOR GOD

✎ *To love God is the first and greatest commandment.*

"'And you shall love the LORD your God with all your heart, with all your soul, with all your mind, and with all your strength.' This is the first commandment."
(Mark 12:30)

"But take diligent heed to do the commandment and the law which Moses the servant of the LORD commanded you, to love the LORD your God, to walk in all His ways, to keep His commandments, to hold fast to Him, and to serve Him with all your heart and with all your soul." (Joshua 22:5)

This is not a suggestion; this is a commandment. This is the greatest and the most important commandment. All other commandments, our faith, and all that Christianity stands for depend on this commandment. We are commanded to actively and diligently love the Lord God with all our heart, soul, mind, and strength. Nothing is more important than this. Everything we do must be linked to this commandment or else we will be in sin.

The implication of this commandment is that our love for God must surpass our love for all else. We are to love other people or things only in reference to God. We must be ready to do whatever it takes to please and glorify Him.

CONFESSION

I love God with all of my heart, with all of my soul, with all of my mind, and with all of my strength. This is the greatest commandment, and I purpose to obey it all the days of my life. I will worship Him and serve Him in spirit and in truth.

🕊️ *It is the grace of God that enables us to love Him.*

Love has been perfected among us in this: that we may have boldness in the day of judgment; because as He is, so are we in this world. There is no fear in love; but perfect love casts out fear, because fear involves torment. But he who fears has not been made perfect in love. We love Him because He first loved us. (1 John 4:17-19)

Now may the Lord direct your hearts into the love of God and into the patience of Christ. (2 Thessalonians 3:5)

I love the LORD, because He has heard My voice *and* my supplications. (Psalm 116:1)

We love God because He first loved us. We love Him because the love of God has been shed abroad in our hearts. To love God with all our heart, soul, mind, and strength is not by our own power or might; it is by the Spirit of the Lord. It requires total dependence on the Holy Spirit.

The Bible says God gives grace to the humble (James 4:6). To walk in real love, we must learn to submit to God. When we submit to God, He will give us the grace to resist the devil and to resist the temptation to put our selfish desires ahead of God's will (James 4:7).

God will not ask us to do something we cannot do with His help. He will not allow us to be tempted beyond what we can bear (1 Corinthians 10:13). If He said for us to love Him with all of our heart, soul, mind, and body, then He has equipped us to do so. He has given us grace, the enablement to perform.

Confession

I can love God with all my heart, soul, mind, and strength because God has equipped me to do so. I can do all things through Christ who strengthens me. It is not by my power; it is by the Spirit of the Almighty God.

☞ *To love God is to minister to the needs of others.*

For God is not unjust so as to forget your work and the love which you have shown toward His name, in having ministered and in still ministering to the saints. (Hebrews 6:10 *NASB*)

If someone says, "I love God," and hates his brother, he is a liar; for he who does not love his brother whom he has seen, how can he love God whom he has not seen? And this commandment we have from Him: that he who loves God *must* love his brother also.
(1 John 4:20-21)

"For I was hungry and you gave Me food; I was thirsty and you gave Me drink; I was a stranger and you took Me in; I was naked and you clothed Me; I was sick and you visited Me; I was in prison and you came to Me." Then the righteous will answer Him, saying, "Lord, when did we see You hungry and feed *You*, or thirsty and give *You* drink? When did we see You a stranger and take *You* in, or naked and clothe *You*? Or when did we see You sick, or in prison, and come to You?" And the King will answer and say to them, "Assuredly, I say to you, inasmuch as you did it to one of the least of these My brethren, you did it to Me."
(Matthew 25:35-40)

One of the ways we demonstrate our love for God is to minister to the needs of others, especially those who are helpless. When you minister to the needs of other people, you automatically minister to God. Jesus said in Matthew 25:31-46 that when we feed the hungry, house the homeless, and clothe the naked we do it directly to Him. You cannot love God and hate your brother at the same time.

CONFESSION

I will demonstrate my love for God by ministering to the needs of others. I will love my neighbor. I will feed the hungry; give water to the thirsty; help the stranger; clothe the naked; and visit the sick and those in prison.

To love God is to keep his commandments.

Whoever believes that Jesus is the Christ is born of God, and everyone who loves Him who begot also loves him who is begotten of Him. By this we know that we love the children of God, when we love God and keep His commandments. For this is the love of God, that we keep His commandments. And His commandments are not burdensome. (1 John 5:1-3)

You who love the LORD, hate evil! He preserves the souls of His saints; He delivers them out of the hand of the wicked. (Psalm 97:10)

But whoever keeps His word, truly the love of God is perfected in him. By this we know that we are in Him. He who says he abides in Him ought himself also to walk just as He walked. (1 John 2:5-6)

"But that the world may know that I love the Father, and as the Father gave Me commandment, so I do. Arise, let us go from here." (John 14:31)

"He who has My commandments and keeps them is the one who loves Me; and he who loves Me will be loved by My Father, and I will love him and will disclose Myself to him." (John 14:21 *NASB*)

Love will always seek to please the one it loves. If we love God as we say we do, we will always seek to please Him. To please God is to obey His Word; it is to keep His commandments.

We must continually evaluate ourselves to be sure our daily activities are pleasing God. At the beginning of each day, we should do a pre-evaluation of the day's schedule: What are the things I am scheduled to do today? Are all of them designed to please the God I love? Will any of the things I am scheduled to do today offend my God?

During the day, we should have an ongoing evaluation of whatever we are doing: Am I pleasing God with what I am doing now? Is this what my Heavenly Father desires for me to do, or is there something else I should be doing? Is this thing I am doing right now breaking any of God's commandments? Can I defend what I am doing now before God or the pastor of my church? Then, at the end of the day we should reevaluate ourselves: Did everything I have done today please God? Which of the things I did today do I need to repent of?

CONFESSION

I love God; therefore, I will always obey His commandments. I will do whatever He asks me to do. I will not walk in disobedience; instead, I will be obedient to all of His commandments.

 To love God is better than sacrifice.

"And to love Him with all the heart, with all the understanding, with all the soul, and with all the strength, and to love one's neighbor as oneself, is more than all the whole burnt offerings and sacrifices." (Mark 12:33)

"But woe to you Pharisees! For you tithe mint and rue and all manner of herbs, and pass by justice and the love of God. These you ought to have done, without leaving the others undone." (Luke 11:42)

To love God is better and more acceptable to God than any offering or sacrifice we may bring to His altar. Sacrifice, offerings, and tithes should be given to God out of a heart that truly loves Him. It is very important that when we bring our offerings and tithes to God, we examine our hearts and our motives, and make sure we are giving to God out of love and gratitude and not out of compulsion or ceremony. Give cheerfully because you love to give.

An offering or tithe given in love is given to God; while an offering, tithe, or seed given otherwise is nothing more than a gift to whomever it is given. Yes, you may receive some blessing from the latter, but it will not be as much blessing as when your motive is the former. In order for you to receive the maximum benefit from your giving, you should give with the right attitude and motive. Evaluate your heart, and get it right before you give.

Confession

To love God with all my heart, soul, mind, and strength is better than sacrifice and offering. I will give my tithe and my offering as a token of my love for Him. I will not give out of a selfish motive but out of love for God, and because His Word instructs me to give tithes and offerings. I will not allow my giving to hinder my love walk.

🐾 *God rewards those who love Him.*

But let all those rejoice who put their trust in You; let them ever shout for joy, because You defend them; let those also who love Your name be joyful in You. (Psalm 5:11)

"I call heaven and earth as witnesses today against you, *that* I have set before you life and death, blessing and cursing; therefore choose life, that both you and your descendants may live; that you may love the LORD your God, that you may obey His voice, and that you may cling to Him, for He is your life and the length of your days; and that you may dwell in the land which the LORD swore to your fathers, to Abraham, Isaac, and Jacob, to give them." (Deuteronomy 30:19-20)

"Therefore know that the LORD your God, He *is* God, the faithful God who keeps covenant and mercy for a thousand generations with those who love Him and keep His commandments." (Deuteronomy 7:9)

But if anyone loves God, this one is known by Him. (1 Corinthians 8:3)

The LORD preserves all who love Him, but all the wicked He will destroy. (Psalm 145:20)

"Because he has set his love upon Me, therefore I will deliver him; I will set him on high, because he has known My name. He shall call upon Me, and I will answer him; I *will be* with him in trouble; I will deliver him and honor him. With long life I will satisfy him, and show him My salvation." (Psalm 91:14-16)

"But showing mercy to thousands, to those who love Me and keep My commandments." (Exodus 20:6)

I love those who love me; and those who diligently seek me will find me. (Proverbs 8:17)

Oh, love the LORD, all you His saints! For the LORD preserves the faithful, and fully repays the proud person. (Psalm 31:23)

God will faithfully reward those who love Him even for a thousand generations. God will defend them. He will fight for them and be a shield over them. For that reason, they can rejoice and be glad knowing fully well that God is on their side. God will give long life to those who love Him and make them to dwell safely and securely.

Because they have set their love upon Him, God promised to deliver them from the snare of the evil one, from pestilences, from attacks of the enemy, and from plagues. God will set them on high and will not allow them to get in trouble. They shall call upon His name, and He will answer them.

God takes special interest in those who love Him. He teaches them and reveals Himself to them so that they can know Him more. Those who love God will grow in spiritual knowledge of God because as they draw near to God, He draws near to them (James 4:8).

CONFESSION

I will rejoice because I put my trust in God. I choose life and not death. I will love my God. I will obey His voice. I will cling to Him. He is my life and the length of my days. I will dwell in the land, which my God has given to me, in peace and in prosperity.

My God is faithful. He will keep the covenant He has with me and the mercy He has for me, unto a thousand generation because I love Him and I keep His commandments.

I have set my love on God. Therefore, He will deliver me. He will set me on high, because I have known His name. When I call upon Him, He will answer me. He will be with me in trouble. He will deliver me and honor me. With long life He will satisfy me and show me His salvation.

GROUP 3
SCRIPTURES TO HELP YOU CULTIVATE LOVE FOR YOURSELF

You are what the Word of God says you are and not what the world says you are. Find out what the Word of God says you are, and make that your daily confession. Feed your heart with those words, and speak them out constantly until they flow out of your mouth naturally anytime you need them.

> "A good man out of the good treasure of his heart brings forth good; and an evil man out of the evil treasure of his heart brings forth evil. For out of the abundance of the heart his mouth speaks." (Luke 6:45)

When you feed your heart with the treasure of God's Word, that will be what will flow out of your mouth when you speak. Jesus is our example. He continually confessed who He was and what His mission on earth was.

> "I am the good shepherd; and I know My *sheep*, and am known by My own." (John 10:14)

> "I and *My* Father are one." (John 10:30)

> *"The Spirit of the* LORD *is upon Me, because He anointed Me to preach the gospel to the poor; He has sent Me to heal the brokenhearted, to proclaim liberty to the captives and recovery of sight to the blind, to set at liberty those who are oppressed; to proclaim the acceptable year of the* LORD.*"* (Luke 4:18-19)

These are some of the things Jesus Christ said about Himself. He never looked to the world to define Himself. Instead, He always declared what the Word of God said about Him. We must do likewise because Scripture teaches that we should be imitators of Christ (Ephesians 5:1). Here are some of the things the Word of God says about you. Feed on these scriptures until they flow out of you naturally.

You are saved by God's Grace and your confession.

But what does it say? *"The word is near you, in your mouth and in your heart"* (that is, the word of faith which we preach): that if you confess with your mouth the Lord Jesus and believe in your heart that God has raised Him from the dead, you will be saved. For with the heart one believes unto righteousness, and with the mouth confession is made unto salvation. For the Scripture says, *"Whoever believes on Him will not be put to shame."* For *"whoever calls upon the name of the LORD shall be saved."* (Romans 10:8-11, 13)

CONFESSION

I believe in my heart that Jesus Christ is the Son of God. I believe He died on the cross for my sins. I believe He was raised from the dead. I confess Him as my Lord and Savior. Jesus, You are my Lord. You are in charge of my life. You will guide me and lead me in the way of righteousness all the days of my life.

You are a child and heir of God and a joint heir with Christ.

For as many as are led by the Spirit of God, these are sons of God. For you did not receive the spirit of bondage again to fear, but you received the Spirit of adoption by whom we cry out, 'Abba, Father.' The Spirit Himself bears witness with our spirit that we are children of God, and if children, then heirs—heirs of God and joint heirs with Christ.... (Romans 8:14-17)

Behold what manner of love the Father has bestowed on us, that we should be called children of God! Therefore the world does not know us, because it did not know Him. Beloved, now we are children of God; and it has not yet been revealed what we shall be, but we know that when He is revealed, we shall be like Him, for we shall see Him as He is. And everyone who has this hope in Him purifies himself, just as He is pure. (1 John 3:1-3)

CONFESSION

I am a child of God. I am an heir of God. I am a joint heir with Christ Jesus. Therefore, I will not fear, neither will I be dismayed because I am a child of the Almighty God.

In God you live and are protected.

"For in Him we live and move and have our being...." (Acts 17:28)

After these things the word of the LORD came to Abram in a vision, saying, "Do not be afraid, Abram. I *am* your shield, your exceedingly great reward." (Genesis 15:1)

CONFESSION

In God I live. In God I move. In God I have my being. Every thing I am and everything I do, I do it through the power of God who created me and who gives me the breath of life. He is my strength, my shield, and my exceedingly great reward.

📖 *Jesus is the vine; you are the branch.*

"Abide in Me, and I in you. As the branch cannot bear fruit of itself, unless it abides in the vine, neither can you, unless you abide in Me. I am the vine, you are the branches. He who abides in Me, and I in him, bears much fruit; for without Me you can do nothing. If anyone does not abide in Me, he is cast out as a branch and is withered; and they gather them and throw *them* into the fire, and they are burned. If you abide in Me, and My words abide in you, you will ask what you desire, and it shall be done for you. By this My Father is glorified, that you bear much fruit; so you will be My disciples." (John 15:4-8)

CONFESSION

Jesus is the vine, and I am the branch. I abide in Christ, and He abides in me. His life and his nature flows through my inner being. Through Him, I am able to bear much fruit: the fruit of love.

📖 *You are a new creation, created in Christ Jesus.*

Therefore, if anyone *is* in Christ, *he is* a new creation; old things have passed away; behold, all things have become new. (2 Corinthians 5:17)

For we are His workmanship, created in Christ Jesus for good works, which God prepared beforehand that we should walk in them. (Ephesians 2:10)

CONFESSION

I am a new creation, created in Christ Jesus for good works. Old things have passed away; all things have become new. I have a new life. I have a new beginning, a new start. All of my past is gone. My sins and my failures; every abuse, addiction, and victimization, which I suffered in the past, are gone forever in Jesus' Name. I have a clean slate, and from today onwards, I am going to live a clean and victorious life through Christ Jesus. Amen.

You are the righteousness of God in Christ Jesus.

For He made Him who knew no sin *to be* sin for us, that we might become the righteousness of God in Him. (2 Corinthians 5:21)

There is therefore now no condemnation to those who are in Christ Jesus, who do not walk according to the flesh, but according to the Spirit. For the law of the Spirit of life in Christ Jesus has made me free from the law of sin and death. (Romans 8:1-2)

For if by the one man's offense death reigned through the one, much more those who receive abundance of grace and of the gift of righteousness will reign in life through the One, Jesus Christ. (Romans 5:17)

CONFESSION

I am the righteousness of God in Christ Jesus. I have no feeling of condemnation because I am in Christ Jesus, and I do not walk according to the flesh but according to the Spirit. The law of the spirit of life in Christ Jesus has made me free from the law of sin and death.

You have the mind and wisdom of Christ.

For "Who has known the mind of the LORD that he may instruct Him?" But we have the mind of Christ. (1 Corinthians 2:16)

But of Him you are in Christ Jesus, who became for us wisdom from God — and righteousness and sanctification and redemption. (1 Corinthians 1:30)

CONFESSION

Jesus Christ lives in me. The Holy Spirit lives in me. Therefore, I have the mind of Jesus Christ. I am able to discern between what is good and what is evil. Jesus Christ is my wisdom; He is my righteousness; He is my sanctification; He is my redemption.

You can overcome because greater is He who lives in you than he who lives in the world.

You are of God, little children, and have overcome them, because He who is in you is greater than he who is in the world. (1 John 4:4)

And they overcame him by the blood of the Lamb and by the word of their testimony, and they did not love their lives to the death. (Revelation 12:11)

CONFESSION

I am an overcomer because the Greater One lives in me. I have overcome by the blood of the Lamb, Jesus Christ, and by the word of my confession.

❧ *You are blessed with all spiritual blessing, and you can do all things through Christ.*

Blessed be the God and Father of our Lord Jesus Christ, who has blessed us with every spiritual blessing in the heavenly *places* in Christ. (Ephesians 1:3)

I can do all things through Christ who strengthens me. (Philippians 4:13)

CONFESSION

God has blessed me with every spiritual blessing in heavenly places in Christ Jesus. I believe that I can do all things through Christ Jesus who strengthens me.

Group 4
Scriptures to Help You Cultivate Love for other People

🔖 *Love for others is the second greatest commandment.*

Jesus answered him, "The first of all the commandments *is*: '*Hear, O Israel, the* LORD *our God, the* LORD *is one. And you shall love the* LORD *your God with all your heart, with all your soul, with all your mind, and with all your strength.*' This is the first commandment. And the second, like *it, is* this: '*You shall love your neighbor as yourself.*' There is no other commandment greater than these." (Mark 12:29-31)

"A new commandment I give to you, that you love one another; as I have loved you, that you also love one another." (John 13:34)

"This is My commandment, that you love one another as I have loved you." (John 15:12)

And this is His commandment: that we should believe on the name of His Son Jesus Christ and love one another, as He gave us commandment. (1 John 3:23)

But concerning brotherly love you have no need that I should write to you, for you yourselves are taught by God to love one another. (1 Thessalonians 4:9)

Confession

I love the Lord my God with all my heart, with all my soul, with all my mind, and with all my strength. I love my neighbor as I love myself. I am a disciple of Jesus Christ; therefore, I will love everyone whom God brings across my path. I will love my fellow Christians and members of the Church just as Jesus loves me. I will be kind and affectionate, honoring and giving preference to all.

Love is the evidence of salvation.

Beloved, let us love one another, for love is of God; and everyone who loves is born of God and knows God. He who does not love does not know God, for God is love. (1 John 4:7-8)

We know that we have passed from death to life, because we love the brethren. He who does not love *his* brother abides in death. Whoever hates his brother is a murderer, and you know that no murderer has eternal life abiding in him. (1 John 3:14-15)

CONFESSION

I am born of God, who is love. Therefore, I walk in love because I have passed from death to life.

Love for other people is evidence that you truly love God.

And this commandment we have from Him: that he who loves God *must* love his brother also. (1 John 4:21)

We love Him because He first loved us. If someone says, "I love God," and hates his brother, he is a liar; for he who does not love his brother whom he has seen, how can he love God whom he has not seen? (1 John 4:19-20)

In this the love of God was manifested toward us, that God has sent His only begotten Son into the world, that we might live through Him. In this is love, not that we loved God, but that He loved us and sent His Son to be the propitiation for our sins. Beloved, if God so loved us, we also ought to love one another. No one has seen God at any time. If we love one another, God abides in us, and His love has been perfected in us. (1 John 4:9-12)

CONFESSION

I will allow God to be seen in me by walking in love.

↬ Real love is sacrificial.

And walk in love, as Christ also has loved us and given Himself for us, an offering and a sacrifice to God for a sweet-smelling aroma. (Ephesians 5:2)

By this we know love, because He laid down His life for us. And we also ought to lay down *our* lives for the brethren. (1 John 3:16)

↬ Faith works by love.

For in Christ Jesus neither circumcision nor uncircumcision avails anything, but faith working through love. (Galatians 5:6)

🌿 *Love is a/the fruit of the Spirit.*

But the fruit of the Spirit is love, joy, peace, longsuffering, kindness, goodness, faithfulness, gentleness, self-control. Against such there is no law. And those *who are* Christ's have crucified the flesh with its passions and desires. If we live in the Spirit, let us also walk in the Spirit. Let us not become conceited, provoking one another, envying one another. (Galatians 5:22-26)

🌿 *Love gives value to the other gifts of the Spirit.*

Though I speak with the tongues of men and of angels, but have not love, I have become sounding brass or a clanging cymbal. And though I have *the gift of* prophecy, and understand all mysteries and all knowledge, and though I have all faith, so that I could remove mountains, but have not love, I am nothing. And though I bestow all my goods to feed *the poor*, and though I give my body to be burned, but have not love, it profits me nothing. (1 Corinthians 13:1-3)

🌿 *These are the distinguishing characteristics of real Love:*

Love suffers long *and* is kind; love does not envy; love does not parade itself, is not puffed up; does not behave rudely, does not seek its own, is not provoked, thinks no evil; does not rejoice in iniquity, but rejoices in the truth; bears all things, believes all things, hopes all things, endures all things. (1 Corinthians 13:4-7)

Confession

I have real love. I endure long. I am patient and kind. I am neither envious nor jealous. I am not vainglorious. I do not parade myself. I am not puffed up. I do not behave rudely. I am not arrogant or inflated with pride. I do not act rudely, unmannerly, or unbecomingly. I do not insist on my own rights or on my own way. I am not self-seeking. I am not touchy, angry, fretful, or resentful. I take no account of evil done to me. I pay no attention to suffered wrong. I do not rejoice at iniquity, injustice, or unrighteousness; but I rejoice in the truth and when right prevails. I bear all things. I believe all things; I am ever ready to believe the best of every person. My hopes are fadeless under all circumstances, and I endure all things without weakening. My love never fails. It will never fade or become obsolete or come to an end. I will walk in love at all times.

⮕ *Love always overcomes.*

Love never fails. But whether *there are* prophecies, they will fail; whether *there are* tongues, they will cease; whether *there is* knowledge, it will vanish away. And now abide faith, hope, love, these three; but the greatest of these *is* love. (1 Corinthians 13:8, 13)

Do not be overcome by evil, but overcome evil with good. (Romans 12:21)

Confession

My love will never fail. I will not be overcome by evil; instead, I will overcome evil with good.

↳ *Love will be remembered.*

Remembering without ceasing your work of faith, labor of love, and patience of hope in our Lord Jesus Christ in the sight of our God and Father.
(1 Thessalonians 1:3)

Let no one despise your youth, but be an example to the believers in word, in conduct, in love, in spirit, in faith, in purity. (1 Timothy 4:12)

↳ *Love must be from a pure heart.*

Now the purpose of the commandment is love from a pure heart, *from* a good conscience, and *from* sincere faith. (1 Timothy 1:5)

Since you have purified your souls in obeying the truth through the Spirit in sincere love of the brethren, love one another fervently with a pure heart.
(1 Peter 1:22)

Let love be without hypocrisy. Abhor what is evil. Cling to what is good. (Romans 12:9)

↳ *Pursue love.*

Pursue love, and desire spiritual *gifts*, but especially that you may prophesy. (1 Corinthians 14:1)

Flee also youthful lusts; but pursue righteousness, faith, love, peace with those who call on the Lord out of a pure heart. (2 Timothy 2:22)

↬ *Put on love, the bond of perfection.*

But above all these things put on love, which is the bond of perfection. (Colossians 3:14)

↬ *Love forgives.*

Therefore, as the elect of God, holy and beloved, put on tender mercies, kindness, humility, meekness, longsuffering; bearing with one another, and forgiving one another, if anyone has a complaint against another; even as Christ forgave you, so you also *must do*. (Colossians 3:12-13)

↬ *Love can abound; love can grow.*

And this I pray, that your love may abound still more and more in knowledge and all discernment." (Philippians 1:9)

And may the Lord make you increase and abound in love to one another and to all, just as we *do* to you. (1 Thessalonians 3:12)

↬ *Love is doing good.*

Let brotherly love continue. Do not forget to entertain strangers, for by so *doing* some have unwittingly entertained angels. Remember the prisoners as if chained with them—those who are mistreated—since you yourselves are in the body also. Marriage is honorable among all, and the bed undefiled; but fornicators and adulterers God will judge. (Hebrews 13:1-4)

And let us consider one another in order to stir up love and good works. (Hebrews 10:24)

Let love *be* without hypocrisy. Abhor what is evil. Cling to what is good. *Be* kindly affectionate to one another with brotherly love, in honor giving preference to one another; not lagging in diligence, fervent in spirit, serving the Lord; rejoicing in hope, patient in tribulation, continuing steadfastly in prayer; distributing to the needs of the saints, given to hospitality. Bless those who persecute you; bless and do not curse. Rejoice with those who rejoice, and weep with those who weep. Be of the same mind toward one another. Do not set your mind on high things, but associate with the humble. Do not be wise in your own opinion. Repay no one evil for evil. Have regard for good things in the sight of all men. If it is possible, as much as depends on you, live peaceably with all men. Beloved, do not avenge yourselves, but *rather* give place to wrath; for it is written, *"Vengeance is Mine, I will repay,"* says the Lord. Therefore *"if your enemy is hungry, feed him; if he is thirsty, give him a drink; for in so doing you will heap coals of fire on his head."* Do not be overcome by evil, but overcome evil with good. (Romans 12:9-21)

But whoever has this world's goods, and sees his brother in need, and shuts up his heart from him, how does the love of God abide in him? My little children, let us not love in word or in tongue, but in deed and in truth. (1 John 3:17-18)

And let us not grow weary while doing good, for in due season we shall reap if we do not lose heart.

Therefore, as we have opportunity, let us do good to all, especially to those who are of the household of faith. (Galatians 6:9-10)

↬ *Love cares about others.*

Let no one seek his own, but each one the other's *well-being*. (1 Corinthians 10:24)

Let each of you look out not only for his own interests, but also for the interests of others. (Philippians 2:4)

↬ *Love covers a multitude of sins.*

And above all things have fervent love for one another, for *"love will cover a multitude of sins."* (1 Peter 4:8)

↬ *Perfect love and perfect Christ-like character brings perfect knowledge of Christ.*

But also for this very reason, giving all diligence, add to your faith virtue, to virtue knowledge, to knowledge self-control, to self-control perseverance, to perseverance godliness, to godliness brotherly kindness, and to brotherly kindness love. For if these things are yours and abound, *you will be* neither barren nor unfruitful in the knowledge of our Lord Jesus Christ. (2 Peter 1:5-8)

Also read and meditate upon the entire first chapter of 2 Peter.

↳ Do all things with love.

Let all *that* you *do* be done with love. (1 Corinthians 16:14)

↳ Love your family sacrificially.

Husbands, love your wives, just as Christ also loved the church and gave Himself for her, that He might sanctify and cleanse her with the washing of water by the word, that He might present it to Himself a glorious church, not having spot or wrinkle or any such thing, but that it should be holy and without blemish. So husbands ought to love their own wives as their own bodies; he who loves his wife loves himself. For no one ever hated his own flesh, but nourishes and cherishes it, just as the Lord *does* the church. For we are members of His body, of His flesh and of His bones. *"For this reason a man shall leave his father and mother and be joined to his wife, and the two shall become one flesh."* This is a great mystery, but I speak concerning Christ and the church. Nevertheless let each one of you in particular so love his own wife as himself, and let the wife *see* that she respects *her* husband. (Ephesians 5:25-33)

That they admonish the young women to love their husbands, to love their children. (Titus 2:4)

꙳ Love strangers.

The stranger who dwells among you shall be to you as one born among you, and you shall love him as yourself; for you were strangers in the land of Egypt: I *am* the LORD your God. (Leviticus 19:34)

"Therefore love the stranger, for you were strangers in the land of Egypt." (Deuteronomy 10:19)

꙳ Love your enemies.

"You have heard that it was said, '*You shall love your neighbor* and hate your enemy.' But I say to you, love your enemies, bless those who curse you, do good to those who hate you, and pray for those who spitefully use you and persecute you, that you may be sons of your Father in heaven; for He makes His sun rise on the evil and on the good, and sends rain on the just and on the unjust. For if you love those who love you, what reward have you? Do not even the tax collectors do so? And if you greet your brethren only, what do you do more *than others*? Do not even the tax collectors do the same? Therefore you shall be perfect, just as your Father in heaven is perfect." (Matthew 5:43-48)

Bless those who persecute you; bless and do not curse. Therefore *"if your enemy is hungry, feed him; If he is thirsty, give him a drink; for in so doing you will heap coals of fire on his head."* (Romans 12:14, 20)

GROUP 5
SCRIPTURES TO HELP YOU RECEIVE LOVE FROM OTHER PEOPLE

▷ *Show yourself friendly.*

A man *who has* friends must himself be friendly, but there is a friend *who* sticks closer than a brother." (Proverbs 18:24)

CONFESSION

I purpose to show myself friendly to other people.

▷ *As you give love, you will receive love in return.*

" Judge not, and you shall not be judged. Condemn not, and you shall not be condemned. Forgive, and you will be forgiven. Give, and it will be given to you: good measure, pressed down, shaken together, and running over will be put into your bosom. For with the same measure that you use, it will be measured back to you." (Luke 6:37-38)

CONFESSION

I will not judge; therefore, I will not be judged by others. I will not condemn; therefore, I will not be condemned by others. I will forgive; therefore, I will be forgiven by others. I will give, and it will be given to me: good measure, pressed down, shaken together, and running over will it be given to me. I will love; therefore, I will also receive love from others.

↳ *Learn to be generous.*

A man's gift makes room for him, and brings him before great men. (Proverbs 18:16)

Confession

I am a generous giver, not so that I can receive from other people, but because it is the right thing to do.

↳ *Pursue mercy and truth. Learn to show mercy and speak the truth in love at all times.*

Let not mercy and truth forsake you; bind them around your neck, write them on the tablet of your heart, *and* so find favor and high esteem in the sight of God and man. (Proverbs 3:3-4)

Confession

I will be merciful to other people. I will speak the truth in love at all times. I will not seek to deceive other people.

Appendix

Daily Confessions

❧ *I am a child of the Most High God. I will be perfect just as my Father in Heaven is perfect; therefore, I will walk in love even if no one else does. I will love my neighbors. I will love my enemies. I will bless those who curse me. I will do good to those who hate me, and I will pray for those who spitefully use me and persecute me* (Matthew 5:43-45, 48; Luke 6:27-28).

❧ *The love of God is poured out in my heart by the Holy Spirit. I have the love of God in me now* (Romans 5:5).

❧ *I have real love. I endure long. I am patient and kind. I am not envious nor jealous. I am not vainglorious; I do not parade myself, and I am not puffed up. I am not arrogant or inflated with pride. I do not behave rudely or unmannerly or unbecomingly. I do not insist on my own rights or on my own way. I am not self-seeking, touchy, angry, fretful, or resentful. I take no account of evil done to me. I pay no attention to suffered wrong. I do not rejoice at iniquity, injustice or unrighteousness, but I rejoice in the truth and when right prevails. I bear all things and believe all things. I am always ready to believe the best of every person. My hopes do not fade under any circumstances, and I endure all things without weakening. My love never fails. It will never fade or become obsolete or come to an end. I will walk in love at all times* (1 Corinthians 13:4-8).

❧ *I love the Lord my God with all my heart, with all my soul, with all my mind, and with all my strength. I love my neighbor as I love myself* (Matthew 22:37-39; Mark 12:30-33; Luke 10:27).

❧ By God's grace, my love will not grow cold. Instead my love will grow stronger in Jesus' name (Matthew 24:12).

❧ I am not a hypocrite. My love is genuine. I hate evil and cling to what is good. I do not have a critical attitude. I do not judge; therefore, I will not be judged. I do not condemn others; therefore, I will not be condemned. I forgive; therefore, I will be forgiven (Luke 6:37, 39-42; Romans 12:9).

❧ I am a disciple of Jesus Christ; therefore, I love. I love all those whom God brings across my path. I love, just as Jesus Christ loves me. I am kind and affectionate to everyone. I honor and give preference to all (John 13:34-35; John 15:12; Romans 12:10).

Therefore, I will not strive, I will not judge, I will not criticize, I will not envy, and I will not be jealous of any person, whether at home, in the Church, in the office, in the school, in the street, or anywhere else. I will love, respect and honor everyone. Man or woman, old or young. I will appreciate them for who they are and for what God has given them.

❧ My Heavenly Father loves me because I love Jesus and believe that He came forth from God. I am abiding in the love of Jesus (John 16:27; John 15: 9-10).

❧ I bless those who persecute me. I bless them instead of cursing them. I rejoice with those who rejoice and weep with those who weep. I associate with the humble, and I am not high-minded. I am not wise in my own eyes (Romans 12:14-16).

❧ I live in peace with all men. I do not strive or quarrel with any person. I do not avenge myself, but rather I overcome evil with good (Romans 12:17-21).

❧ *I love the government of my country of birth. I also love the government of my country of residence. I pray for those in authority and I obey the laws of the land* (Romans 13:1-7).

❧ *I owe no one anything except to love them* (Romans 13:8).

❧ *I walk in love; therefore, I make sure my actions do not grieve anyone* (Romans 14:15).

❧ *I have knowledge, but I am not puffed up by my knowledge. Instead, I do everything I can to edify my neighbor* (1 Corinthians 8:1).

❧ *I pursue love. I do all things and say all things in love* (1 Corinthians 14:1; 1 Corinthians 16:14).

❧ *I have a sincere love for God and for everyone* (2 Corinthians 6:6; 8:8).

❧ *The God of love and peace is with me* (2 Corinthians 13:11,14).

❧ *My faith works by love* (Galatians 5:6).

❧ *I love my neighbor as myself* (Galatians 5:14).

❧ *The fruit of the Spirit is love. I walk in the Spirit, and I bear the fruit of love* (Galatians 5:22).

❧ *As I walk in love, I will be holy and blameless before God* (Ephesians 1:4).

❦ *I have love for all the saints* (Ephesians 1:15).

❦ *Christ dwells in my heart through faith, and I am rooted and grounded in love. I know the love of Christ, which passes knowledge, and I am filled with all the fullness of God* (Ephesians 3:16-19).

❦ *I will walk worthy of the calling with which I have been called with lowliness and gentleness, with longsuffering, bearing with one another in love; I will endeavor to keep the unity of the Spirit in the bond of peace* (Ephesians 4:1-3).

❦ *I speak the truth in love* (Ephesians 4:15).

❦ *I will imitate my Father God. As a sacrifice, I will walk in love as Christ loved me and gave Himself for me* (Ephesians 5:1-2).

❦ *I love my wife just as Christ loves the Church and gave Himself for it. I will nourish my wife and cherish her just as the Lord does the Church* (Ephesians 5:25-33).

❦ *I am joined to my spouse and we are one flesh. I love my spouse, and I am not bitter toward him or her* (Colossians 3:18-19).

❦ *I put on love at all times, which is the bond of perfection* (Colossians 3:14).

❦ *I labor in love* (1 Thessalonians 1:3).

❦ *The Lord makes me to increase and abound in love in Jesus' name* (1 Thessalonians 3:12).

🕊 *I am of the day and of the light, and I put on the breastplate of hope and love* (1 Thessalonians 5:8).

🕊 *God has not given me a spirit of fear, but of power and of love and of a sound mind* (2 Timothy 1:7).

🕊 *I pursue righteousness, faith, love, and peace* (2 Timothy 2:22).

🕊 *I will stir up my love and good works* (Hebrews 10:24).

🕊 *I am of one mind with the Body of Christ. I have compassion for others. I have love for my brothers and sisters in the Lord. I am tenderhearted and courteous toward them* (1 Peter 3:8).

🕊 *I have fervent love for all of my brethren. I cover others' sins, and I do not expose them* (1 Peter 4:8).

Prayer of Salvation

Dear God, I recognize that I have sinned against You and against other people. Please forgive my sins. I repent of them. I believe in my heart that Jesus Christ was crucified for my sins. I believe in my heart that You raised Him from the dead. I confess with my mouth that Jesus is Lord. He is my Lord and my Savior. Jesus, You are my Lord and my Savior.

Come into my heart Lord Jesus. Fill me with Your Holy Spirit. Create in me a clean heart and a renewed and steadfast spirit. Cast me not away from Your presence. Restore unto me the Joy of Your salvation. And help me to love You with all of my heart, with all of my soul, with all of my mind, and with all of my strength in Jesus' Name I pray.

Thank You, Father God, I believe that from now on I am a new creature. I am created in Christ Jesus for good works. From now on, God is my Father, and I will live for You all the days of my life. In Jesus' Name, Amen.

If you prayed the above prayer, you are born again. From now on, diligently seek the Lord and learn to receive His love for you. You are now the righteousness of God in Christ Jesus. That means your old sinful nature and your past sins have been purged, and you have been given a new nature, a new spirit—a spirit that is alive to God.

> Therefore, if anyone *is* in Christ, *he is* a new creation; old things have passed away; behold, all things have become new. Now all things *are* of God, who has reconciled us to Himself through Jesus Christ, and has given us the ministry of reconciliation, that is, that God was in Christ reconciling the world to Himself, not imputing their trespasses to them, and has committed to us the word of reconciliation. Now then, we are ambassadors for Christ, as though God were pleading through us:

we implore you on Christ's behalf, be reconciled to God. For He made Him who knew no sin to be sin for us, that we might become the righteousness of God in Him. (2 Corinthians 5:17-21)

If you are not presently attending church, go and find one where you feel welcome. Tell the pastor or one of the associates that you have recently accepted Jesus as your Lord. They will guide you appropriately. Also, please feel free to write us a letter or send us an email, and we will send some materials that will help you in your Christian walk. Our address is located on the copyright page of this book.

NOTES

Chapter 1
[1]Warren W. Wiersbe, *The Bible Expository Commentary* (Wheaton, Illinois: Victor Books, 1989). Electronic edition copyrighted 1996, by SP Publications. Accessed in Libronix Digital Library System), Commentary on 1 Thessalonians, "Chapter Six: How to Please Your Father (1 Thessalonians 4:1-12)." [Note: This reference applies to all the statements made in this paragraph.]

Chapter 2
[1]*Cambridge Advanced Learner's Dictionary*, 2nd Edition (2005), s. v. "love."

[2]Warren W. Wiersbe, *The Bible Expository Commentary* (Wheaton, Illinois: Victor Books, 1989. Electronic edition copyrighted 1996, by SP Publications. Accessed in Libronix Digital Library System, Commentary on 1 Thessalonians, "Chapter Six: How to Please Your Father (1 Thessalonians 4:1-12)."

[3]Warren W. Wiersbe, _____ Commentary on 1 Thessalonians, "Chapter Six: How to Please Your Father (1 Thessalonians 4:1-12)."

[4]Thayer and Smith. "Greek Lexicon entry for Philarguros". "The New Testament Greek Lexicon". http://www.studylight.org/lex/grk/view.cgi?number=5366, (23 June 2006).

[5]Thayer and Smith. "Greek Lexicon entry for Thelo". "The New Testament Greek Lexicon" http://www.studylight.org/lex/grk/view.cgi?number=2309, (23 June 2006).

[6]*Vines's Complete Expository Dictionary of Old and New Testament Words (1996)*, s. v. "love."

[7]Thayer and Smith. "Greek Lexicon entry for Philandros". "The New Testament Greek Lexicon". http://www.studylight.org/lex/grk/view.cgi?number=5362, (24 June 2006).

[8]Thayer and Smith. "Greek Lexicon entry for Philoteknos". "The New Testament Greek Lexicon". http://www.studylight.org/lex/grk/view.cgi?number=5388, (24 June 2006).

[9]Vines, 382

Chapter 3
[1]Thayer and Smith. "Greek Lexicon entry for Makrothumeo". "The New Testament Greek Lexicon". http://www.studylight.org/lex/grk/view.cgi?number=3114, (26 June 2006).

[2]*Nelson's New Illustrated Bible Dictionary* (1995), s.v. "envy."

[3]Gill, John. "Commentary on 1 Corinthians 13:5". "The New John Gill Exposition of the Entire Bible". http://www.studylight.org/com/geb/view.cgi?book=1co&chapter=013&verse=005> . 1999. (20 July 2006).

[4]Gill, John. "Commentary on 1 Corinthians 13:7"

[5]Adam Clarke, "Commentary on 1 Corinthians 13," "The Adam Clarke Commentary," http://www.studylight.org/com/acc/view.cgi?book=1co&chapter=013, 1832, (19 December 2006).

[6]Adam Clarke, "Commentary on 1 Corinthians 13,"

Chapter 4
[1]Thayer and Smith. "Greek Lexicon entry for Hebdomekontakis". "The New Testament Greek Lexicon". Http://www.studylight.org/lex/grk/view.cgi?number=1441>, (14 August 2006)

[2]H. Wayne House, *Chronological and Background Charts of the New Testament* (Grand Rapids, MI: Zondervan, 1981), 27.

Chapter 7
[1]Austin-Sparks, T. *His Great Love.* Forest Hill, London: Witness and Testimony Publishers, ___.

Chapter 8
[1]Marvin R. Wilson, *Our Father Abraham: Jewish Roots of the Christian Faith* (Grand Rapids, Michigan: William B. Eerdmans Publishing Company and Dayton, Ohio: Center For Judaic-Christian Studies, 1989), 309-310.

Chapter 9
[1]Steven K. Scott, *Mentored by a Millionaire: Master Strategies of Super Achievers* (Hoboken, New Jersey: John Wiley & Sons, 2004), 18-19.

[2]Billy Joe Daugherty, *You Are Valuable* (Tulsa, OK: Victory Christian Center, 1991) 13-24. [This minibook was a valuable resource in the captioning of this bullet point, as well as in the discussion that follows].

[3]Ruthanne Garlock, *Fire In His Bones: The Story of Benson Idahosa.* Tulsa, Oklahoma: Praise Books, 1981.

Chapter 10
[1]Thayer and Smith. "Greek Lexicon entry for Eulogeo". "The New Testament Greek Lexicon". http://www.studylight.org/lex/grk/view.cgi?number=2127, (17 December 2006)

Chapter 11
[1]Henri J. M. Nouwen, *In the Name of Jesus: Reflections on Christian Leadership* (New York, NY: The Crossroad Publishing Company, 1989), 38.

Peter Osagbodje Ministries
(P.O.M.)

OUR PURPOSE

We exist on earth as ambassadors of Jesus Christ, committed to preaching the Gospel of salvation and making disciples of all nations (Matthew 28:18-20; Mark 16:15-18; Luke 24:46-49; John 20:21-23; Acts 1:6-8).

OUR VISION

Our vision is to see people walk in the Christ-given abundant life. That is a life that has a personal relationship with God (salvation); is progressively being transformed into the image of Christ; is in good health; has a good, healthy relationship with family and with others; is financially secure; is actively seeking to be a blessing to other people; and is equipped for the work of the Kingdom.

OUR MISSION

Our mission is to:
- ❖ Preach the Gospel of Salvation to all people wherever they reside.
- ❖ Teach the Truth—the Word of God—with integrity, clarity, and simplicity.
- ❖ Pray for the healing of the sick through the power of the Holy Spirit.
- ❖ Equip the saints for the work of the Kingdom.
- ❖ Encourage and guide people to worship God daily.

OUR AREA OF RESPONSIBILITY

In general, we are called to take the uncompromising Word of God to the unreached people of the world, more specifically, to the villages, towns and cities where people have limited access to the full Gospel.

For more information, additional copies of this book, or donations to our ministry, please write to:

Peter Osagbodje Ministries
P.O. BOX 700971
Tulsa, OK 74170
USA

or Email:
posagbodje@yahoo.com